ALL
JOKES
ASIDE

ALL JOKES ASIDE

STANDUP COMEDY IS A PHUNNY BUSINESS

A MEMOIR

RAYMOND LAMBERT WITH **CHRIS BOURNEA**

FOREWORD BY CHRIS GARDNER

BOLDEN

AN AGATE IMPRINT

CHICAGO

Author's Note

This is a work of nonfiction. I have described the events truly and honestly just as I recall them. To anyone I did not recall or omitted, I offer my sincere apology. While circumstances and conversations depicted herein come from my recollection of them, they are not meant to represent precise timelines or exact word-for-word reenactments of my life. They are told in a way that evokes the real feeling and meaning of what was said, and my view of what happened to me, in keeping with the mood and spirit of those moments that shaped my life.

Copyright © 2016 by Raymond Lambert

All rights reserved. No part of this book may be reproduced or transmitted in any form or by any means, electronic or mechanical, including photocopying, recording, or by any information storage and retrieval system, without express written permission from the publisher.

Printed in the United States

Library of Congress Cataloging-in-Publication Data

Lambert, Raymond C.
All Jokes Aside : standup comedy is a phunny business / Raymond Lambert and Chris Bournea.
    pages cm
Summary: "A behind-the-scenes memoir about Chicago's comedy club All Jokes Aside, which helped launch the careers of many well-known African American entertainers"-- Provided by publisher.
ISBN 978-1-932841-95-4 (pbk.) -- ISBN 1-932841-95-4 (pbk.) --
ISBN 978-1-57284-763-7 (ebook) -- ISBN 1-57284-763-8 (ebook)
1. All Jokes Aside (Chicago, Ill.) 2. Stand-up comedy--Illinois--Chicago--History. I. Bournea, Chris. II. Title.
PN3166.C55A55 2015
792.7609773'11--dc23
                    2015021251

10 9 8 7 6 5 4 3 2 1   16 17 18 19 20

Bolden is an imprint of Agate Publishing. Agate books are available in bulk at discount prices.

agatepublishing.com

To Nia Rae and Maya Jo Jo:
Your daddy loves you

CONTENTS

Don't give me a fish; don't even teach me how to fish! Teach me how to own the pond—then I can fish whenever I like.

—TUDOR BISMARK

FOREWORD
BY CHRIS GARDNER

IN THE EARLY 1990S, I was grooming a young investment banker named Raymond Lambert to help me expand my brokerage firm, Gardner Rich & Company. Raymond was bright, ambitious, self-motivated, and a fast learner, able to think on his feet and come up with a workable solution to pretty much any challenge that came at him.

So you can imagine my shock, hurt, and anger when Raymond announced he was leaving my firm to focus full time on the side business he'd started while working for me—a comedy club known as All Jokes Aside. What was he thinking?

I often joke that I'd never hire another Morehouse man again, even if it were Martin Luther King. But the truth is, with the benefit of two decades of hindsight, I admire what Raymond set out to accomplish. Along with his business partner, James Alexander, Raymond created an independent enterprise that not only added value to the highly competitive Chicago comedy market but also became a national pipeline for some of the most talented comedians ever to gain the spotlight.

Another joke of mine is that I was one of the initial investors in All Jokes Aside—without even knowing it. Funny things happen in the markets all the time, but not *that* funny. Raymond would be sitting at his desk, cracking up. He was my top producer, so I left him alone. I didn't know that he was on the phone with Mike Epps, Cedric the Entertainer, D.L. Hughley—all while I was paying him. It's funny now, but it wasn't funny back then. I have to say, in all honesty, that Raymond worked his tail off to build a franchise from the ground up—just as I did with my own business.

All Jokes Aside created something that's still desperately needed in the Chicago marketplace. There are no real venues that ever replaced what All Jokes Aside provided: that entertaining, comfortable space where young talent could expose itself and we could appreciate and share it.

Who knew back then when we were sitting in that club what would happen to that guy onstage? That guy named Jamie Foxx?

Or that guy named Dave Chappelle?

And that guy named Steve Harvey?

Who knew?

And that space in Chicago? There's a void. Some folks would say there's a void coast to coast, but in Chicago, there's a void that's never been filled. If All Jokes Aside were to open its door today, there would once again be a line around the block, and I'd be the first person in it.

CHRIS GARDNER, *New York Times* bestselling author of *The Pursuit of Happyness*, is an internationally known entrepreneur and motivational speaker, as well as Raymond Lambert's former boss.

1

BETTING ON BLACK

I woke up in an ambulance. And it wasn't nothing but white people staring at me. I said, "Ain't this a bitch? I done died and wound up in the wrong mothafucking heaven."

—RICHARD PRYOR

I WAS ONLY 30 IN NOVEMBER 1991, but it already felt like my life was over.

Me and my business partner and college buddy, James Alexander, were out of cash, had maxed out our credit cards, and were behind on our payments to James's mother, who had loaned us $100,000 to realize our dreams of going into business for ourselves. Three months earlier, we had opened All Jokes Aside, Chicago's first and only comedy club geared specifically toward showcasing African American comedians and serving the black community. Opening All Jokes Aside was one of the proudest moments of my life. I could finally call myself an entrepreneur.

But now the club was on the verge of closing. And it wasn't funny.

When James and I first set out to open All Jokes, we were psyched. It was the dawning of a new decade—the go-go '90s—and we liked to think of ourselves as enterprising young mavericks with a hot new idea. In their hit song "Jazz (We've Got)," hip-hop pioneers A Tribe Called Quest summed up our swing-for-the-fences mentality: "It's 1991 and I refuse to come wack. . . ."

All Jokes Aside was an experiment, one of the first of its kind in the nation—a sort of comedy-club version of the popular urban clothing line For Us By Us (FUBU). When we opened All Jokes in 1991, it was a year before HBO's *Def Comedy Jam* and BET's *Comic View* hit the airwaves. And there were no comedy clubs in Chicago that regularly featured black comedians nor any that catered to black customers.

All Jokes Aside was designed to draw African American Chicagoans with disposable income—all 1 million of them—and provide them an opportunity to escape with a good laugh and to relieve the stress of living just enough for the city. If the experiment worked, James and I could launch a new enterprise: the first national chain of black-owned comedy clubs. I had a vision of opening All Jokes Aside comedy clubs in every major market across America.

If the experiment failed, the loss would be devastating for me and James—professionally, financially, and emotionally. For me, a failure on such a grand scale would have resulted in the loss of not only my life savings and that huge investment from James's mother but also my reputation in the business world and any shred of motivation to succeed outside of the narrow confines of Corporate America. If All Jokes Aside had shut its doors at that pivotal moment in November 1991, I would have been on the verge of bankruptcy, even homelessness.

I grew up working class. I paid my own way through college and graduate school. I didn't have much of a financial safety net at the time. While I certainly had the emotional support of family and a lot of great friends I'd met along my journey, I didn't have, to paraphrase Billie Holiday, rich relations to give a crust of bread and such.

If I failed, I was largely on my own.

The situation looked pretty bleak. We had bounced so many checks to vendors that we had to start paying in cash. And we were two weeks behind in our rent on the space we leased to house All Jokes Aside.

So bringing in Steve Harvey, a rising comic at the time, for a weekend of headlining shows was a big deal. Even though Steve was relatively unknown in the early '90s (compared to his superstardom today), he was establishing a reputation at mainstream clubs like the Funny Bone. And even back then, he was expensive—his asking price was triple our standard pay. The average headliner at the time—even Bernie Mac— was only getting $500 to appear at All Jokes. By the time James and I finished our negotiation with Steve, he'd made us feel like he was giving *us* a deal. I hoped that maybe this guy could help us turn the corner—I thought, *He's gotta be good because he's so expensive.*

Booking Steve at such a high cost was like going to the casino with money you'd set aside to pay your mortgage and crossing your fingers that the odds were in your favor. All

Jokes needed an infusion of capital—*fast*—and if the club couldn't make money with a cutting-edge comic like Steve at the top of the bill, it was time for me and James to reassess whether to cut our losses.

We went to our accountant, Vicki Hudson, for advice. A veteran of startups, she told us in no uncertain terms that we should quit. "I demand that you cease and desist," she said. "You've been at this for six months, and you are averaging 75 people a night in a 300-seat venue—and half of them are friends and family. You are $100,000 dollars in debt, all of your accounts are overdrawn, your credit cards are maxed out, you have to pay for everything in cash—which, by the way, you don't have—and you are ruining your personal credit. It was a nice idea, but keep your day jobs."

Despite this harsh dose of reality, James and I vowed to give it one last shot by bringing in Steve. And if this show wasn't a success, we would have to take Vicki's advice and close.

Thank God Steve didn't request a deposit on his pay. Our travel agent floated us a plane ticket. As cash flow was a major issue, James and I couldn't exactly afford to put Steve up in five-star accommodations. And the lodging problem was exacerbated by the fact that a major convention was in town, so hotel rooms were at a premium.

Running our business on a shoestring budget had always forced us to be creative. So James and I put our heads together and came up with a solution: we would put Steve up in a "comedy condo." After all, it was a common industry practice for nightclubs to rent condos to board guest performers who were in town for a few days—hence the term "comedy condo."

The fact that the All Jokes Aside comedy condo happened to be James's personal residence was, I guess, the punchline.

James and I had everything riding on the assumption that having Steve's name on the marquee would help us sell enough tickets not only to cover his fee but also to make a sizable profit and finally get us the exposure we needed to really launch the business. But, of course, we didn't tell Steve we didn't have his money up front. We didn't want to look like amateurs—even though we were.

Before starting the club, neither James nor I had any kind of background in running a real business, especially one in the entertainment industry. We had no experience with managing employees, dealing with the fickle tastes and preferences of audiences, or working with comedians. Neither did our good friend Mary Lindsey, whom we brought on to help out with administrative matters. And none of us knew anything about politics, unions, or liquor licenses. If you were to pick a group to start a comedy club, you certainly couldn't have found a less likely trio.

But everything would work out, right? Just as James and I had gambled that a black comedy club would be in demand among an underserved customer base, we'd also gambled that Steve was a show-business trouper who would do whatever was needed to ensure that the show would go on.

Even if it meant sleeping on James's couch.

Though we did not have a hotel room for Steve, at least James's building was relatively rich in amenities. He was in Presidential Towers, which was a modern apartment building with retail stores, restaurants, a gym, and a spa on the ground floor. It *looked* like a hotel.

Neither of us owned a car, so James borrowed one from a friend and, at my insistence, went to the car wash and cleaned it up good before going to the airport to pick up Steve. We had to appear that we knew what we were doing every step of the way. I was holding my breath and praying that James would not fuck this up, but to be honest, James was the better man for the job. There are a few things I'm bad at, and topping the list are driving and delivering bad news.

Seeing James pull up, Steve was a bit surprised. He had been expecting a limo or, at the very least, a car service. But he seemed to be a good sport about being picked up by one of the club's owners, so after a bit of small talk, James felt it was a good time to discuss the night's lodging situation.

"I have one more small favor to ask," he said. "There are no hotel rooms available in the city tonight, but I have room at my place, and I think that you will like it."

Steve's friendly demeanor quickly faded, and he snapped, "Pull the car over!" They were driving from O'Hare on the expressway, one of the busiest freeways in America. Pulling over was not an option. Paying no attention to the bustling airport traffic, Steve kept ranting: "What do you mean they don't have any hotel rooms? This is Chicago! They got rooms! You don't want to pay for the room, but they got rooms. What's up?"

After a very uncomfortable pause, Steve added, "If you guys weren't black, I'd tell you to take me right back to O'Hare right now, but we're gonna do this. But just let me tell you, next time I come here, there better be a hotel."

When they arrived at James's apartment, James offered to sleep on a cot he had set up so Steve could take the bed. Instead, Steve insisted on taking the cot, propping his ever-present hat on his chest and muttering, "Ain't this some bullshit?"

Though he was still on his way up in his career, roughin' it was not something Steve Harvey was accustomed to at this point—especially since he had established a reputation as one of the sharpest dressers in comedy. He pressed his own clothes and was the first person I'd ever seen who put his shoes and socks on first and *then* his pants—open-casket *sharp*. With his attention to detail, it's not surprising that Steve now has his own clothing line.

Steve's appearance was so important to him that after camping out on James's couch, he got up at the crack of dawn to iron his clothes before a radio appearance I had lined up. To promote his show at All Jokes, Steve was going to be interviewed on the *Doug Banks Radio Show*, one of the hottest urban morning programs in the nation, which happened to be based in Chicago. And we had to be at the radio station by 6 a.m.

I had worked out an arrangement with WGCI-FM that for a fee, All Jokes performers would appear on Doug's show and publicize their engagements at the club. Meeting WGCI's general manager, Marv Dyson, had been one of those proverbial lucky breaks. I'm a firm believer that luck is when preparation meets opportunity, and this was a prime example.

I came across the promotional opportunity with WGCI while talking about All Jokes Aside with my dear friend Noreen

McClendon. At the time, she was a paralegal, and in her spare time, she was helping us draw up contracts with comedians and vendors. I mentioned that I wanted to get my comedians on the air, but the cost to run a radio advertising schedule was more than we were making in a week. "Why don't you call Vida's dad?" she suggested.

As it happened, Noreen and I had been friends with Vida Dyson since our college days at the Atlanta University Center. I was at Morehouse while Noreen and Vida were attending Clark College. Noreen was from Philadelphia, which is a 20-minute train ride from my hometown of Wilmington, Delaware. In short, we were homies.

So Noreen said, "Marv runs a radio station in Chicago and I'm sure he'd welcome the opportunity to meet you." So I did a bit of cursory research, pre-Google style, and asked around about Marv Dyson and WGCI.

I discovered that WGCI was owned at the time by media conglomerate Gannett—best known as the publisher of *USA Today*—and was not only the top station in the Chicago market but also one of the top-rated stations in the nation. Marv was a well-respected veteran and a pioneer in black radio. So I'm thinking, *Oh, shit! What do I have to offer him?*

Knowing I had to do something to draw more ticket buyers to All Jokes, I set my trepidation aside and called Vida. She said, "He would love to meet you. I will call him right now and set it up." She literally called me back in 10 minutes and connected me with Marv.

I knew Marv was an astute businessman when he told me to come by the next day after the stock market closed for the day, which meant he had done a bit of research on me as well. I prepared thoroughly to ensure that I put my absolute best foot forward. In one of my favorite scenes from the hit film *Wall Street*, the hero is standing outside Gordon Gekko's office before finally getting to meet him. He looks at himself in the mirror and says, "Life all comes down to a few moments. This is one of them." I felt that my meeting with Marv would be one of those moments for me.

I stayed up late that night rehearsing my pitch. I went to the station in my best suit, shirt, and tie, and I had my shoes shined on the way to his office. I also brought him a bottle of Scotch. I had been taught to always bring more to the table than an appetite and a spoon. Luckily, at the club, we had a few bottles that distributors had left for us to sample. I knew nothing about Scotch, so I just brought Marv the one with the fanciest label.

I had never been to a radio studio, and it was fascinating. Like almost everyone at that time, I had listened to the radio constantly while growing up. As a high school student deciding what I wanted to be when I grew up, I had even considered broadcasting as a career, and I knew the names of all the deejays. Being at the studio was *very* cool. All the deejays, producers, and behind-the-scenes folks were around. Walking by one area, I remember thinking, *Hey, is that Tom Joyner? Get the fuck outta here!* It was, in fact, Joyner, who garnered his nicknames as "The Fly Jock" and "The Hardest-Working Man in Radio" from an eight-year stint of hosting both a morning show on KKDA-FM in Dallas and an afternoon show on WGCI, to which he commuted by air.

So for me, getting a behind-the-scenes look at the magic of radio was an added benefit to meeting with Marv. When I got to Marv's office and reached out my hand, prepared for a firm handshake, he was like, "Man, give me a hug. Nice tie! Back in the day, you would have taken it off and given it to me!" I'm thinking, *Should I really give it to him? Is this payola?*

Marv invited me to have a seat and explain my situation. So I told him the story and filled him in on what we were trying to build. He got it right away. "What about your day job?" he asked.

"I want to be an entrepreneur and I can do both," I replied.

He said, "Okay," and never asked me about it again.

This was before the now-common practice of having comedians as deejays' on-air sidekicks. Comics, unless they were film or TV stars, were rarely given the opportunity to be on the radio. This was a new idea. I explained that we shared the same demographic as the radio station and I had a plan that would work well for the both of us. I'd bring my comedians on to the Doug Banks morning show, he'd get a funnier show, and I'd get on-air promotion. Win-win!

The only problem was Marv didn't see it that way.

He told me, "If you're getting paid, your publicist is getting paid, the club's getting paid. Why should we give you free exposure on the radio?"

I wanted to shout, "But I'm *not* getting paid! Don't be fooled by the suit and tie. I'm about to be homeless. I'm losing my ass!"

Marv offered to make a deal. We could bring the comedians who headlined at All Jokes Aside on Doug's show for a fee of $500 per appearance. Before responding, I paused, considering his offer. I was thinking, *Five hundred dollars?! Nobody pays for interviews!*

Some small-business owners, especially those with cash-flow problems, would have choked at the notion of forking over $500 per appearance to help WGCI fill air-time. But then again, this was the number-one station in the market. Not just the black market, the *entire* market. They could charge $500 per minute or more for a one-minute ad spot, and we'd be on for at least five minutes. That was a no-brainer. *Done.*

I figured the radio deal would help raise All Jokes's profile—and we needed all the help we could get. This was before Twitter, before Facebook, before Instagram. Black people got most of their entertainment-related information by word of mouth and the radio.

Looking back, this was an instance when having a business degree, rather than a background as a nightclub promoter, may have been an asset. Rather than thinking like a tight-fisted club owner looking for every opportunity to save a buck, I was thinking like the Wall Street bond salesman that I was, who knew the potential payoff of a calculated risk.

I saw the WGCI deal as an investment. Marv told me that I was the first person who realized that this "pay to play" kind of deal made sense. He told me that a lot of the comedy clubs in Chicago flat-out refused to pay to have their performers interviewed on the radio. All Jokes was the only club that took advantage of Marv's offer.

As the meeting wrapped up, I thanked Marv profusely and invited him to a show, which he graciously declined. "Don't worry about paying now," he said. "You can bring the payment with you when you bring the comic. Cashier's check. Let me know ASAP when you want to start."

Why'd he insist on a cashier's check? Because we were a new business? Did I look desperate? Did I look broke? Thank God I didn't have to pay that day, because we were NCF—no cash flow.

So I said, "If it's okay with you, we will start next week." Done. We hugged again and I left. James and I both got paid on the 15th of the month, so that would give us the cash we needed to pay for the radio spot. We booked all of our big shows on the first and the 15th because that was not only when we got paid by our day jobs but also when most of our potential customers got paid, including welfare recipients.

So Steve Harvey's interview on the Doug Banks show was the centerpiece of our last-ditch effort to save our struggling business.

Steve would go on to become a standup sensation, not to mention a television and radio star and bestselling author. You don't get to that level by being unsure of yourself. And in standup comedy, you're going to get nowhere fast if you're afraid to speak up. And speak up is exactly what Steve did when Doug attempted to usher him off the show after the five-minute segment was up. As far as Steve was concerned, he had come too far and endured too much to go off quietly into the night—er, morning.

Steve told Doug—on live radio—that he hadn't come to the station just to be on for a hot minute. Steve insisted, "I got up at 4:30 in the morning after sleeping on the couch, then pressed my clothes out, got here at 5:30, waited in the greenroom until 7, and after five minutes, you finna kick me out? I am the funniest person in this booth! I don't know what jokes you tellin', Doug, but they ain't as good as my material. So I'm staying."

Of course, when Steve pulled this stunt, he hadn't bothered to consult me beforehand, and I was the one who had driven him to the station. So I was literally in a panic. As time ticked away while we waited for Doug's reaction to Steve's dare, my stomach tied itself up in knots. Steve's on-air challenge to Doug caused a scene in the studio. Radio station employees, including Marv himself, came out of their offices to see what all the commotion was about.

I pissed myself. But I stayed put in the booth, wondering if Marv and Doug would kick Steve and me out. Would the new relationship with WGCI that I had so carefully cultivated collapse in these few fateful seconds on the air?

Fortunately, radio stations, like comedy clubs, rely on the public. The phones rang off the hook with callers clamoring to keep Steve on. He ended up staying on Doug's show for another hour.

It certainly didn't hurt that Doug had visited All Jokes and was a supporter of the club and its mission to provide an outlet for African American talent. Partly because he was fond of All Jokes, I think, Doug let Steve stay on over his allotted time. And besides, Steve was damn funny. He was a natural on the air.

Everyone at WGCI, Marv included, cracked up at Steve's antics—much to my relief. But this high-stakes poker game wasn't over yet. My livelihood was still on the line.

Since James and I were chauffeuring Steve around during his visit to the Windy City, I had to remain at WGCI as long as he was on the air. James had already reported to work at his day job at Continental Bank, but I was risking my job at investment firm Gardner Rich & Company in order to stay by Steve's side. I was supposed to be at work at 7 a.m., but by now it was 8:30 a.m.—the same time the stock market opens.

But the risk paid off. I was late to work, but I was able to keep my day job—for the time being, at least. And thanks to Steve basically taking over Doug's show for the morning, buzz for his All Jokes engagement spread. There were long lines to get into Steve's shows. It was incredible. And to accommodate the frenzied demand for tickets, everyone had to pitch in. And, mercifully, Steve's willingness to be a team player was as big as his mouth.

Steve had warned James and me to be prepared for an onslaught and to have someone ready to take reservations and sell tickets as soon as he got off the air. But we had chalked that up to Steve's bravado. We had never needed to do that before. We didn't take reservations; All Jokes was first come, first served. Besides, we had never sold out a show before. We had one phone line connected to an answering machine that gave callers the information for that night's show.

Steve insisted that we go back to the office and check on the phones. He was right. The phone was blowing up. Steve volunteered to work the phone himself, taking reservations and fielding calls from eager ticket buyers. He was truly in it to win it.

I really didn't want Steve to see our "office" at All Jokes. We were renting space at an art gallery. While the room with the stage was beautiful, our office was not. Imagine a walk-in closet with a telephone—that was our office.

But things were about to change, big time. Steve's headlining engagement was a hit, helping All Jokes to gain the momentum we needed to become *the* place to see black comedians who were on the way up. To meet Steve's fee and turn a profit, we needed to sell out every ticket to every show. And we did.

It helped that before Steve took the stage, Chicago natives Bernie Mac and George Willborn, who served as the program's host, warmed up the hometown audience. The show had the feel of a big event, with the audience and the comics alike dressed to impress amid the gallery's upscale décor.

Everything was hitting on all cylinders. That's when James and I knew this thing was viable. We may not have had the money to make a go of it initially, but this club was now hot. As it turned out, a few more cats had to sleep on the couch: Jamie Foxx, Joe Torry, Ricky Harris, and Bill Bellamy, to name a few. But for the most part, after Steve, we were off and rolling.

And fortunately, Steve got a big career boost out of the whole experience as well. As it turned out, that appearance on the *Doug Banks Radio Show* was the start of a long and fruitful career in radio. The station invited him back several times to sit in for Doug, which jumpstarted Steve's broadcasting career. Eventually, WGCI gave Steve a job as the morning-drive host.

Steve's gig with WGCI was ahead of its time. In 1991, Doug Banks only occasionally had comedians on as guests. And when comedians did appear, it was only for a few minutes. Just as he would soon become a trendsetter in fashion, Steve was also a trailblazer in broadcasting. Tom Joyner and comedian J. Anthony Brown—another regular at All Jokes Aside—didn't become nationally syndicated until 1994. And it would be two decades before yet another All Jokes headliner, D.L. Hughley, would host his own nationally syndicated radio show.

Steve Harvey, of course, is now a household name, welcomed every day into living rooms and cars across America as the host of his own top-rated, nationally syndicated morning radio show and Emmy-winning television talk show.

And it all started with that radio spot to promote his standup act at All Jokes Aside.

2

MIRACLES ON 28TH STREET

When I ask how old your toddler is, I don't need to hear "27 months." "He's two" will do just fine. He's not a cheese. And I didn't really care in the first place.

—George Carlin

I was born on June 10, 1961, my father's 19th birthday, in Wilmington, Delaware. I was given his first name, Raymond, and I think the reason why we couldn't get along when I was coming up is that we were so much alike.

He and my mother, Theresa "Patsy" Patterson, got married after I was born. My conception had come as a surprise to the teen lovers, who had thought they were being careful enough to prevent such an "accident."

When my mom found out she was pregnant with me, most of her family and friends told her, "Why would you have a kid at 17? You are smart enough to go to college. Why don't you have an abortion?" Rumor has it that they went with her to an abortion clinic, but she never got out of the car. She told them, "I just can't do it."

I often say that's where I got my persistence. I was coming here for a purpose, one way or another.

As Snoop Dogg once said, if you were raised in the '70s, in the "neighborhood," you probably have seen a man and a woman in a fistfight. The man—if you want to call him that—didn't always come out on top. But in my parents' altercations, the sheer force of Raymond Walter's fiery disposition usually dominated. My parents exchanged vows, but being so young, they were not really ready to raise a family. In fact, my mom was still in high school, so jumping into a big commitment at such a young age was stifling. In a sense, they felt like their lives were over before they truly began. I believe this led to my mother's eventual retreat into alcoholism and to my father's deep bouts of depression, which in turn fueled fits of rage.

Much of my mom's despair stemmed from a "dream deferred," to quote Langston Hughes. She always wanted to go to New York, and people always thought she would make a good model. She dropped out of Howard High School in order to have me.

My mom turned to alcohol to self-medicate; it was a way out. Though she never mentioned her dreams or hopes to me, I did and still do internalize the notion that I, in some small way, contributed to her alcoholism. Of course I didn't, but a sense of guilt resides in me to this day. My life's objective was always to make the world a better place for her, to provide for her all that she hoped and dreamed of. Beginning at age 10, with the money from my various ventures—paper delivery, lawn care, snow removal—I'd buy her gifts and flowers. Entrepreneurship always seemed like the best way to be able to do that.

While my father didn't overindulge in alcohol, rage was his drug of choice. The volatile combination of his temper and my mom's drinking sometimes led to physical altercations. My mother was no punk and took shit from nobody, but my father was usually the one who would start the fight.

Then he'd turn his attention to me. My father used his hand, a switch, a belt, a club, whatever was within reach to "discipline" me and my younger brother, Nevan. It was because of my father's physical abuse that when I became the parent of two girls, I decided I would never use corporal punishment. I believe it is a practice that has its roots in slavery, and it needs to end. Discipline can be done effectively without beatings. I cringe every time I see a parent doing so.

But in my household growing up—as was the case in many households within the black community "back in the day"—the father was the disciplinarian. To spare my brother and me from our father's wrath after we violated some rule, whenever she could, my mom would take us into a room, close the door, and pretend to beat us. She was drawing on her untapped acting skills, and so was I! Had our "performances" been recorded, I would have been nominated for an Oscar. We would both laugh so hard in-between my hollering and screaming that we'd be worn out when we emerged from a "beating."

I remember one occasion in particular, though, that was far from funny—my father took me into my bedroom and "spanked" me with an extension cord. That shit has to be worse than waterboarding! After about two minutes, I noticed the bedroom door was cracked, so I grabbed the cord, pulled him down, and bolted out of the room. You were never supposed to grab the "belt"; that only extended the ass-whooping. But I was in such pain that I was willing to take my chances.

Once I escaped my father's grip, I ran down the street wearing only my T-shirt, tighty-whities, and tube socks. I ran for at least half a mile before I stopped. I didn't care what my friends, neighbors, or complete strangers thought—I was literally running for my life. Getting whipped with an extension cord hurts. *Bad.* In an odd way, it's funny in the telling now, but it certainly wasn't funny then.

Eventually, I made it to my mom's parents' house and sought the protection of my grandmother. When my grandmother saw the state I was in, she was enraged. She really let my father have it. Strangely, she never intervened on my mother's behalf, but that time, she was not having it. I did not get another beating for weeks.

My parents' violent episodes upset my little brother and me, but domestic violence was a relatively common occurrence in the neighborhood where I grew up. While the yelling, hitting, and chaos in my household was unsettling, I understood, even as a kid, that our family wasn't unique. I knew several families in my neighborhood where there was domestic violence. I knew it wasn't right, but it wasn't unusual. When you get old enough to know, you suppress it and never talk about it to anyone. You only hope that one day it will end—peacefully.

I'm still angered by my father's behavior. And even as a kid, I was at a loss as to why my mother's family didn't intervene and take a more active role in standing up for their sister. My maternal uncle, Sonny Patterson, whom I remain close with to this day, said he always viewed my parents' rocky marriage as a matter that should be kept between them.

"I never got into their private business," Uncle Sonny told me recently. "They were young when they got married."

Uncle Sonny said my father would sometimes confide in him about his and my mother's problems. Uncle Sonny would listen, but he left it up to my parents to work things out on their own.

The fact that my father always held down two or three jobs may have been the source of some of the tension in the household. Because my father worked so much, my mom was able to be a stay-at-home mom when my brother and I were little. But the traditional arrangement left her wanting more.

"I think she was more or less bored," Uncle Sonny said.

Much later, I learned that stress from being an overworked teen parent shouldering the responsibility of being the sole breadwinner was not the only reason Raymond Walter was often on edge. My father was eventually diagnosed as manic-depressive and was prescribed medication. My brother and I had grown up and left the house by then, and the long-overdue diagnosis came too late for us to be spared our father's volcanic moods. My dad was a deeply troubled and complicated person.

Things changed dramatically, however, when I was 14. At that age, I was the same size that I am today and in peak athletic condition. When my dad came at my mom one day, I rope-a-doped him, and at one point, I pushed him off her and into a wall—*hard*—with both of my hands around his throat. That was the last time he approached my mother or me physically. They divorced shortly thereafter.

Unlike my doting maternal grandparents, I don't think that my father's parents were too happy about me. My father was the middle child of 13 children—no sets of twins—and I think that he had been viewed as the one with the most promise to break the cycle of poverty. He was the one who had the ability to take it to the next level: college, engineer, something. Now here I come.

As a preteen, I spent a little time with my Grandma Sadie and Grandpop Norman at their farm in Marshallton, Delaware. Sadie had been born in Richmond, Virginia. Her mother, my great-grandmother, was a "Black Indian," the descendant of a Native American and a runaway slave. I am descended from people who didn't wait on their freedom, they ran for it.

My grandfather was originally from Coatesville, Pennsylvania. I was so impressed that he had built his house with his own hands. Early on, my grandparents raised their own animals and grew their own fruits and vegetables. With 13 kids, you gotta do that. With so much competition for scarce resources, my father got in the habit of eating his dessert first, which he did even when I was growing up. If you didn't get dessert first in a family of 13 kids, there would only be crumbs left by the time the cake, pie, or other sweets made it around the table.

I can't say that I ever really enjoyed my infrequent visits to Marshallton. I certainly loved the Lamberts and hung out occasionally with my aunts, uncles, and cousins who lived in Wilmington. But in Marshallton, there was just as much chaos in their house as there was in my own. My paternal grandparents often got into physical altercations. It wasn't unusual for police to be called to their house; they knew them by name.

When I was born, my mom still lived with her parents, William and Lucille Patterson, who lived at 2614 North Pine Street. My grandparents had arrived in Wilmington from Florida in the 1930s during the Great Migration.

My maternal grandparents were the steadying force in all of our lives. My grandfather worked in the warehouse at the Speakman Company, a manufacturer of plumbing products. I remember my grandfather as one cool dude. William Patterson was tall, charming, and strikingly handsome. I used to love to watch him get dressed. He would twist his belt buckle to the side, button his shirt up to the top button, and display a crisp handkerchief in his back pocket—I myself still carry one daily. He'd also put water in his straight hair and comb it through so effortlessly. I tried to do that, but the kinks got in the way. What was up with that?

I later learned that my grandfather was biracial, the product of a white mother and a black father—thus, the straight hair. This was unacceptable in 1910, so he was dropped off at an orphanage immediately after his birth. He never knew either of his parents.

What I remember most about my grandfather is that he *loooooooved* my grandmother. It's hard to describe, but even as a child I just felt the love, admiration, and respect. She was indispensable to us all. Lucille Patterson made a lasting impression on me. She was not only the matriarch of the family but also the adult I looked up to most as a role model.

My mom was literally a child when she had me, and though I always respected her as my mother, she often seemed more like the older sister that was in charge when the mother wasn't around. My grandmother was more of the traditional mother figure for me. She pretty much shaped my whole philosophy on life. She was what Dr. Maya Angelou was talking about in the poem "Phenomenal Woman." If I could have dinner with just one person, dead or alive, it would be my grandmother—no contest. She was the most dedicated, hard-working, loving, intelligent, immaculately dressed, selfless person that I have ever met.

My grandmother's parents hailed from Kingston, Jamaica, and immigrated to Jacksonville, Florida, as migrant farm workers. They were no strangers to backbreaking work. My grandmother picked fruits and vegetables long before Mexicans began doing more of this field labor. She and her parents came all the way up the coast and finally settled in Wilmington.

Though she only had a third-grade education, Lucille Patterson was more intelligent, articulate, and business-savvy than most of the MBAs I have come to know. She made it seem effortless to tend to my grandfather and their seven children, run her business with excellence, and keep a spotless home—a home they owned. You could eat off the floor, any day, any time with no advance notice. I never heard the phrase, "Let's clean up because company's coming over," until I was an adult because our houses were always white-glove clean.

My grandmother worked as a domestic, and her clients were often prominent white families. One of the perks of her business was that she "inherited" designer clothes and furnishings that wealthy society ladies passed on when they cleaned their closets in preparation for the next fashion season. I'm sure Lucille Patterson was the only person in our neighborhood wearing a Chanel suit at the bus stop on her way to work. And it looked like it was made for her. She looked like she stepped out of the pages of *Vogue*. You can't buy class.

Probably the greatest lesson I ever learned from my grandmother was attention to detail. Some of my fondest memories were going with her to the farmers' market and watching how she meticulously sought out the best fruits, vegetables, and meats. The vendors knew her and would often reach under the counter or go to the back to get the best stuff for her. And they celebrated her approval. Or they quickly tried to appease her disapproval with other options—and these were white people. I learned to never settle for less than the best that your money could buy.

Even as a kid, I admired the way she handled her business. She carefully selected her clients rather than relying on kindly white folks to hire her. She ran her own show on her own terms in a day and age when many African Americans struggled just to make ends meet. And the clients loved her. While they summered in places around the globe, they would send her gifts. I remember most the fruits and vegetables sent to her from California and Florida. Those were exotic places to me. My grandmother would say, "When you grow up, you'll visit those places. Be sure to take me with you!"

She died when I was 14 years old. As fate would have it, I had a job selling flowers outside the hospital where she died, so I got to take her flowers every day that she was there. I have never met another human being like her. I doubt that I ever will.

Despite the household turmoil, I have relatively good memories of my childhood overall. My family, particularly my mother's family, was where I got much of my work ethic and my sense of style. Where I came from made me who I am today.

When my father was honorably discharged from the army following two years of service—only a year before the ramp-up to Vietnam began—we moved from my grandparents' house to an apartment on Spruce Street. He found a job as a spotter at a dry cleaner, which didn't pay much. Our little family's first apartment was a step above a tenement. My mom kept our place spick-and-span, but our neighbors? Not so much. Despite our best efforts, if you turned the lights on quickly at night, you'd see a few roaches scatter.

Even with the meager accommodations, Spruce Street was fun. I had lots of friends and we'd run the streets for hours. Most importantly, Spruce Street is where I met Mr. Frank Crawford, my self-appointed godfather. An entrepreneur, he was a bail bondsman by trade who also wrote a sports column for the local African American newspaper. Initially, I think he was fond of my mother and used me to try to get closer to her. That didn't work out for him because she was hopelessly devoted to my father, but he grew very fond of me.

I learned so much from Mr. Crawford about people, manhood, sports, business, and life in general. None of his kids seemed too interested in what he did, but I was enthralled. One of the things I remember most about Mr. Crawford was that he always wore a freshly pressed custom-made suit with a crisp white shirt, a fresh carnation, and Stacy Adams shoes. *Gangster*. His shoes were so polished that they looked like mirrors. He dressed like that every day. And whenever he'd pick me up for the day, our first stop was the barbershop for a haircut and shave.

Mr. Crawford always had a pocketful of cash and took me everywhere with him: jails, police stations, court, and a few other places where an eight-year-old shouldn't have ventured. Mr. Crawford taught me a lot about the criminal mind and the bail bonds business. I'm convinced that if Mr. Crawford hadn't died before I came of age, I would have taken over that business. He believed in me and often asked me what I thought about a particular situation. I loved learning about his business and that aspect of society.

After two years of living on Spruce Street, my dad got a new, higher-paying position as an apprentice in the machine shop at the DuPont Company and took on a second job. We were able to move to a better neighborhood. As a military veteran, my dad used the GI Bill to purchase a two-flat—a duplex where we lived in the bottom and rented out the top— on East 28th Street. *Moving on up*. It was a working-class neighborhood located two blocks (and two paychecks) from the projects. The neighborhood was 99 percent black. The only white families in my neighborhood were the folks who couldn't afford to move. People took pride in their homes, and we looked at it as *our* neighborhood. Everyone took care of his or her piece, and that made the pie good.

My mom taught me to read and write before I went to school so I was academically prepared. And she let me walk to kindergarten on my own while she tended to my newborn baby brother, Nevan. It was maybe six blocks. I felt all grown up. Unbeknownst to me, she watched me the whole time.

After we moved to our new apartment, I attended George Gray Elementary School, a public school that had a mix of working-class kids and students from the public housing development across the street. Like many African Americans, I soon became "bilingual"—well versed in the informal lingo of the projects as well as the more formal language of mainstream society.

It was at George Gray Elementary that I had lessons, both academically and in life, from one of my favorite teachers and one whom I consider to be among the best ever: Ms. Closson for third grade. Ms. Closson was "Afrocentric" before the term existed. She had a close-cropped Afro, wore colorful dashikis and clogs, and did not take any shit from anybody—especially us kids. She drilled us on our history and insisted that we prepare ourselves to change the world, even though we were only in third grade!

Ms. Closson wasn't shy about doling out discipline, physical or otherwise. I remember one incident when a classmate nicknamed "Little Eddie" and I decided to square off in a cursing contest at recess. I was only eight at the time, but I knew all the words and how to say them because my parents cursed like sailors when they fought. Little Eddie also had a vocabulary well beyond his years. He was from the projects, and kids from the projects grow up a little faster. I'm reminded of one of my all-time favorite bits by the late, great Bernie Mac: "The word 'mothafucka' is a noun. It describes a person, place, or thing. You might see four or five brothers together and you might hear the word 'mothafucka' 32 times. And you might just hear two regular English words, but the conversation makes sense like a mothafucka." That was Little Eddie and me on the playground that day.

When Little Eddie and I returned to Ms. Closson's classroom after recess, she called me to the front of the class. Before I knew it, she had me in a headlock with her knuckles in my head. Tears welled up in my eyes, but she had nothing on my dad—I was more embarrassed than hurt. And Lord knows I was not going to tell my parents. Back then, you sucked it up and prayed that your parents never found out or that would be another ass-whooping.

While she had me in a headlock, Ms. Closson said, "This is not acceptable behavior for a young man. You are a leader, not a follower." All I could manage to get out was, "Yes, ma'am, I'm sorry." I never cursed at school again.

Increasingly, I invested my time and energy outside of the classroom in sports, especially football and basketball. It gave me a reason not to be at home and have to deal with all of that chaos. And I loved it. Making the basketball team at Brown's Boys Club changed my life. Brown's Boys Club is where I learned the true value of hard work, motivation, self-control, resilience, dedication, discipline, teamwork, and the significance of winning. Coaches Gil Jackson and Rich Johnson exerted a major influence on me. They taught me lessons not only about basketball but also about life— lessons that I carry with me to this day. Coach Jackson was a proud member of the Kappa Alpha Psi fraternity, and that was a major factor in my later pledging Kappa at Morehouse.

It was around this time that I began to idolize New York Knicks legend Walt "Clyde" Frazier. His book, *Rockin' Steady: A Guide to Basketball and Cool*, became my bible. Obsessed, I carried it with me everywhere I went. I even slept with it under my pillow. Reading it under the night-light is probably why I wear glasses today. It showed you everything—like the Magna Carta of cool: how to dress and how to carry yourself on and off the court. I idolized Frazier so much that in high school, my nickname became "Clyde."

On the Brown's Boys Club basketball team, we would practice every day for two or three hours. There was a lot of running. The coaches' philosophy was, "Our competition may be more talented, but they're never going to outwork us, and they're never going to be in better condition than us. And fatigue makes cowards of us all. We will play man-to-man defense, full court, for the entire game. I promise you that by the fourth quarter, they're going to be drained. And that's when we kill them." We probably ran 10 miles a day or more—and we were only 12 years old!

I am always taken aback when juvenile athletes today are handed trophies just for showing up and patted on the back for participating, lest their fragile self-esteem suffer any damage. At Brown's Boys Club, we had no such comforts. Every year, dozens and dozens of cats would show up to try out. Half would quit the first day because the physical demands of the practices were so brutal. Our coaches didn't even bring out a ball until probably the fourth practice. All we did were running and defensive drills. These were shouting, scream-in-your-face coaches: John Thompson and John Chaney types. And I loved it. No parent dared step into the gym other than on game day. And even then, the parents kept their opinions to themselves. How are you going to argue with success?

We never accepted second-place trophies. You don't win second place; you lose first place. Ribbons for good sportsmanship? Not in our team's world. We were about perfection. We might not get there, but it wouldn't be from a lack of effort. I recall having practice after a game—a game that we won by 30 points! Those lessons have stuck with me throughout my life. Work hard, seek perfection, and persevere. Practice does not make perfect; perfect practice makes perfect. I later translated that mindset of excellence at all costs to the business world. I wanted All Jokes Aside to be the best comedy club in the world. Not the best black comedy club but the best comedy club, period. And for a brief period in time, I think it was.

I would continue to learn the value of teamwork while playing basketball in high school. But I wasn't a great student. That would come back to haunt me. I was just smart enough to have a few options. And my father was committed and willing to offer me opportunities to get the best possible education in high school. Like many African Americans who wanted to provide a high-quality education for their children in the 1960s and '70s, my father saw private school as the way to accomplish that goal. So he offered me the opportunity to attend Salesianum High School, a Roman Catholic, independent, all-boys prep school that is still one of the top private institutions in the country. The Catholic Education

Honor Roll named Salesianum one of the top 50 Catholic high schools in America every year from 2007–2010.

In 1950, Rev. Thomas Lawless, OSFS, a legendary principal at Salesianum and a member of the first four-year graduating class in the school's history in 1907, admitted five African American students. This was four years prior to the *Brown v. Board of Education* decision that ended school segregation. Salesianum was the first racially integrated school in the state of Delaware.

Salesianum also has a venerable history of powerhouse athletics. Its trophy case displays an impressive 149 state championships in total. There is a plaque in the gymnasium training facility that sums it up nicely: "Since its inception, Salesianum has been home to the sons of working-class families from Wilmington. It welcomed ambitious young men who desired a rigorous Catholic education and instilled them with Salesian values. Many students refined these values on the playing field in athletic competition in preparation for championing them as Salesian gentlemen throughout their lives."

I was confident that I could do well at Salesianum, where I could pursue my love of sports but also where academic excellence was expected. If I just stayed focused and worked hard, I could maybe even earn a college scholarship. My father believed in me and wanted me to have opportunities. And he was willing to work three jobs in order to pay the tuition.

But it took me a while to adjust. Growing up, I went to predominantly black schools, but at Salesianum, the student body's racial makeup was completely flipped.

Every day, I had to make a 1.5-mile walk through my neighborhood, where I was taunted for wearing a shirt and tie to attend my predominantly white prep school. It got to a point where I stopped wearing my tie out of the house and would not put it on until Salesianum was in sight. On several occasions, I was late for school, and in my haste, I forgot my protocol and found myself in front of my locker with no tie. Always right there to remind me was Willard "The Father" Razinski, the dean of students. Forgetting a tie earned you a demerit.

I was experiencing culture shock. The language, the style, the food, everything was foreign to me. *Mac and cheese for lunch? That's it? What the fuck? That's a side dish. Where is the rest of the food?* Hell, I had never even had a white teacher before. During my time at Salesianum, there were no black teachers—the school's only black employee was the janitor.

This was the late '70s, the tail end of the Black Power movement. And I was developing a very Black Nationalist consciousness. Between my Uncle Sonny and the guys at my barbershop, which was owned by Nation of Islam members, I was becoming, in the words of Richard Pryor, "ultra black." I spent hours debating my friends about ideas and philosophies on slavery, civil rights, the Black Panther Party, the current condition of black folk, and "The Man." Through these debates and my uncle's informal lectures that I heard every two weeks at the barbershop, I was developing a strong sense of black identity.

I often went to the barbershop even when I didn't need a haircut. There, school was in session. I was a voracious reader and the men there recommended plenty of books and periodicals. I didn't just study the material—I slept with the books and papers they gave me under my pillow, reading what I could under the night-light. I read all the time and everywhere. At one point, my mother banned me from bringing books to the dinner table, so I snuck them on my lap and ate slowly, staying in place until everyone else had left the table so I could read. I devoured the works of Harriet Tubman, Frederick Douglass, Booker T. Washington, W.E.B. DuBois, Marcus Garvey, Paul Robeson, J.A. Rogers, Martin Luther King, Muhammad Ali, and James Brown. Yes, *that* James Brown. The Godfather of Soul is one of the most underrated civil rights leaders in history. I was also an avid follower of Malcolm X. *The Autobiography of Malcolm X* changed my life.

As you might imagine, these kinds of ideas did not always go over well at Salesianum. I was not militant but introspective. I would always think things through before I spoke, but I wasn't a guy who was going to go along with things just because that's the way they were. I had no problem expressing my views in class or anywhere else. I was not going to blindly follow doctrine. I had been taught to question everything and everybody. And besides, I was attending Salesianum because of its academic and athletic reputation, not because of my religion.

Religion was not a major part of my childhood—quite the opposite. Church is the pillar of the community and the center of family life for many African Americans, but I was never forced to attend any religious venue other than school. I don't even recall going to any funerals held at churches; those were always at funeral homes.

Growing up, I got the sense that my parents felt most religious people were hypocrites. My mother used to repeat a story over and over again about how she went to church once and saw the pastor's wife drinking liquor straight out of the bottle in the bathroom. To my complete surprise, my mother would later find Jesus and embrace the church.

My father never expressed an interest in religion. He believed, as I do, that people should find faith of their own accord, not be pushed into it by a parent or anyone else. Expose your kids to all that is out there and let them decide what's best for them. He did, however, always say that the black church was very good at the hereafter, but the "here now"... not so much.

But while no one religion was dominant in our family, I had family members and friends who were atheist, Baptist, Muslim, Buddhist, Jehovah's Witness, and Seventh-day Adventist. You name it, I was exposed to it. We would debate religion and philosophy for hours. The debates were most intense at the barbershop.

I could relate to what the Black Muslims were saying: "Black people are not catching hell because we are Muslim or Baptist or Jehovah's Witness; we are catching hell because we are black." While I did not always agree with them entirely, they did speak truth to power. And I liked that. A lot.

So I came up with this brilliant idea to speak truth to power at school. I'd show these priests at Salesianum what the deal was. What the "truth" was. What they were missing. How they had it all wrong.

I studied other religions and read the Bible and other texts so I could find things that in my mind were illogical, disputable, or contradictory. One time I came across a passage from Matthew 23:9: "Call no man father but the Father. . . ." While I generally refused to interpret the Bible literally, I took this passage to heart, and on one occasion, I refused to call the priests "Father."

"It says so in the Bible, right here," I argued. "Please explain."

The response I got was, "I don't have to explain anything to you, lad. Demerit."

"Okay, but let me ask you this: Was Jesus black?"

Demerit.

"How about Adam and Eve?"

Demerit.

"Do animals have souls? Do they go to heaven?"

"No."

"Then what do people eat in heaven? Are they vegetarians?"

Demerit. Demerit.

Needless to say, my acts of rebellion earned me numerous acts of contrition. I earned so many demerits that one time, I had to go to detention every day for a week *and* over the weekend. Freedom of speech can be expensive!

I was not much better at home. I stayed in trouble. Not criminal stuff but more relatively minor infractions like violating curfew. If the time I had to be home made no sense to me and I felt it was unreasonable, I ignored it fully, content to suffer the consequences. The benefits of staying out past curfew outweighed the punishment I'd receive. I needed to be in the streets with the people! Being home by midnight was just too early, not enough time for me to find and teach all of the lost souls. Not to mention the pretty girls. I needed to be out until at least 2 a.m. After all, it was the weekend. My pops wasn't having it.

"I don't give a fuck what's happening in them streets!" he'd yell at me. "You better have your ass in here by midnight."

My pops would try to wait up for me, watching the door to monitor if I'd make curfew, but he'd usually fall asleep. For a while, I could reach my hand in the door and unhinge the lock and let myself in quietly. He'd wake up perplexed, but since he'd fallen asleep, he wouldn't know what time I'd gotten in. He'd ask, "What time did you get home?" I'd reply with a straight face, "Twelve, sir."

But soon he wised up and changed the locks. So I had to change my strategy. I'd knock on the window and my brother would let me in. After a few times of that, my father turned up the heat on my brother. He threatened Nevan with the same punishment he'd give me if he let me in. My brother folded like a deck of cards.

I suffered many a cursing-out and beating, and ultimately, I was locked out of the house several nights and had to sleep on the front lawn.

Other than religion class and a few other classes that held my interest, I didn't really apply myself during my first few years at Salesianum. I just wanted to play ball and get outta there. I didn't really do homework, although I did pay close attention in class. But, laugh at me as you might, this was all part of a master plan. You had to have a 2.0 grade point average to play ball, and I wanted to do a little better than that.

So my goal was a 2.1. What's the point of doing more than is necessary? I was black and a jock; nobody had high expectations of me, anyway. Right?

In spite of my lackadaisical attitude toward authority and academics, for three seasons I played basketball and, during the off-season, held down a part-time job. I worked at Juice O Mat, a health food store that was like a precursor to Whole Foods, GNC, and many of the organic markets that are fairly commonplace today but weren't exactly on every street corner back in the '70s. Mr. Ryan, the owner of Juice O Mat, taught me most of what I know about healthy eating. I learned about the benefits of a vegetarian diet and various supplements—many things that I still practice to this day. I was learning to nourish my body, but my home life continued to be unhealthy. My parents continued to fight. I became numb to it, but my brother, four years younger, would often cry himself to sleep. The chaos carried on until 1977, when my parents finally decided to divorce. I was only 15 when they split up, but I was beyond relieved.

I hated the side of my father that treated my mother that way. And I was disappointed in her for not packing us up and breaking camp a long time ago. It took me 30 years to come to grips with the idea that maybe—and not in a way that justified their actions—their discord resulted from the frustration of having kids as teenagers and feeling like their dreams were crushed before they even had a chance to live their lives. It's one thing to have a dream die of its own weight; it's another thing altogether to never have the chance to pursue your dreams in the first place.

After my parents split, my dad remained a strong presence in our lives. And when he realized I was putting my future in jeopardy by not taking school seriously, he set me straight.

By my junior year at Salesianum, I had racked up 19 demerits—just one shy of the magic number that would get me expelled. My parents were summoned to the school.

I don't know how it is in other communities, but in the black community, if your parent has to take a half-day off work to come to your school because you are acting a fool, that's an ass-whipping guaranteed. The only question is how intense it will be. In the parent-teacher conference, Father Razinski suggested that despite my athletic prowess, he felt that it would be better for me to transfer to a public school. I was just not "Salesianum material." He said I would do better in a school with fewer rules, a school that was not as academically rigorous. Hell, the way he put it, I started thinking the same thing.

There was no way my father was going to stand for me wasting the money he worked three jobs to earn. Here's what my father told me after that parent-teacher conference: "I don't give a fuck what Father Razinski is talking about. You are going to that goddamn school and you are going to graduate. I am not going to stand by and let you waste my hard-earned tuition money and throw away the private-school education that I worked so hard and sacrificed so much to provide for your ass. What the fuck is wrong with you?

"Do you think I like going to work and taking shit from white people all day? Do you? I'll give you the short answer: hell no, I don't. I hate it. Every day. But I go and I bust my ass so that you can have the opportunities that I did not. Get your shit together or I'll kill you. I brought you in this world and I will take you out. I mean that."

Then he said, "I am taking you off the team." This was right before the basketball playoffs in my junior year, and I was coming into my own athletically. But despite pleading from the coach and a few other well-meaning parents, my pops said no. I missed the playoffs. We lost.

That was all the incentive that I needed. I finally got it. I vowed to get my shit together and do my best both academically and athletically. In my senior year, I made honor roll several times. Coach Angelo Rossi gave me the keys to the team and trusted me to serve as the coach on the floor. I even scouted other teams and wrote up comprehensive scouting reports. We were Catholic League champs and I made the All–Catholic League team. I led the league in assists and steals and ranked among the top 10 in the state for both statistics. This accomplishment was especially meaningful to me. As a point guard, I had to know everybody else's position and what they were supposed to be doing. Coach Rossi would tell me, "It's your show; run it." Taking on this leadership role helped me later in business; I understood that I had to know what everybody's role was and how to delegate work.

Despite my accomplishments in athletics, I never felt comfortable socially at Salesianum. I never attended one social event during my years there, not one: no dances, no proms, not even the annual sports banquet. I regret that. Straddling two worlds can be tricky.

When it became time to start thinking about college, I knew that after four years of being in the minority, I wanted to learn more about my own history and culture. Not only did I want to attend a historically black institution, I also wanted to get away from home. I applied only to colleges that were at least an eight-hour car ride from Wilmington.

I had overtures from a few schools to play ball and I even got a call from a coach at Villanova. My backcourt mate, Tracy Peal, was an All-American, and I made him look good. But I knew that I was not pro material, and I was not interested in playing simply for the love of the game. What's the point? If I can't operate at the highest level in whatever it is that I am doing, I move on and find some place that I can. I turned my attention to academics. It was then that I realized that I had not done the work that I should have to put myself in a position to attend a top college. I began to realize that I had blown a wonderful opportunity by not putting in the time and effort to take advantage of all that Salesianum had to offer.

My dad would always say, "As a black man, you must work twice as hard for twice as long for half as much. And if you don't remember anything else that I am telling you, remember this: you will never get the benefit of the doubt. Never. So make that shit decisive." I finally got it. I vowed in that instant never to slack off again. I promised myself to take advantage of each and every opportunity and to always do my best. But it was very late in the game. Thank God for Salesianum's stellar staff and reputation.

We also had a highly regarded college placement office and top-tier counselors headed up by Mr. Stephen DiPietro. He painstakingly assisted me throughout the application process and provided me with the same level of attention as the students that were applying to Ivy League schools. One day, I read an article in *Ebony* about Morehouse College in Atlanta, Martin Luther King Jr.'s alma mater, and that became my No. 1 choice.

I remember it like it was yesterday. It was a Tuesday afternoon one fine March day, sunny and unseasonably warm. Mr. DiPietro called me into his office, saying he had a letter for me from Morehouse. I almost fainted because it was a letter-sized envelope. I had been told that only rejection letters came in letter-sized envelopes. Acceptance letters came in big, glossy envelopes with brochures, maps, and all that other stuff.

I opened it and the first sentence read, "Congratulations, you have been accepted to Morehouse College." I cried like a baby. In that instant, I became the first person in my family to go to college.

3

DEAR OLD MOREHOUSE

I celebrated Thanksgiving the old-fashioned way. I invited everyone in my neighborhood to my house, we had an enormous feast, and then I killed them and took their land.

—JON STEWART

AFTER GRADUATING FROM SALESIANUM, I had to work two jobs and go to summer school to prepare for college. Morehouse required that I take a few classes prior to my first semester to tighten up my math and writing skills. My father had paid my high school tuition, so I would have to pay for college. I would have to work every summer and part time during the school year in order to pay the tuition and fees. I had a night gig at Star Janitorial, but I needed a well-paying day job. I found it at Bank of Delaware.

Salesianum has a college and career fair, where colleges and companies from all over the country come and spout the benefits of attending their college or working at their companies. I found Bank of Delaware by pure luck. I had decided that I wanted to be an agent or manager, either for athletes or entertainers, so an opportunity to learn banking would give me a competitive advantage.

I stopped by Bank of Delaware's table, picked up their promotional materials, and talked to the recruiter about their commercial lending program. The program was held every summer and led students through the entire operation of the bank, from the mailroom, to the teller stations, to one day becoming a commercial lender. I was psyched and decided to apply.

So I got home, started doing my cursory research, and on the first page I looked at, I saw a photo of my teammate Larry Corrigan's father. Underneath, it read, "Larry Corrigan, president." *What the fuck?* I had been playing with Larry Jr. for three years. I'd see his dad at many of the games. Larry Jr. and I were tight—on the court, at least. It was one of those things: On the court, we'd kill for each other; Off the court, well, with the exception of Patrick McGinty, my best friend on the team, I never went to any of my white teammates' homes, and they never came to mine.

The next day at school, I ran up to Larry and said, "Dude, your pops is the president of Bank of Delaware!" Larry was a tough-as-nails starter in both football and basketball. He had no interest in banking. I told him I was applying for an internship at his dad's bank.

I applied for the job, and about a week later, I got a call to come in for an interview. I walked in dressed in a blue suit, white shirt, yellow tie, and highly polished black shoes. I needed this damn job. I went up to the human resources department and was greeted like a rock star. I was then taken to a huge corner office that felt bigger than our apartment.

"Raymond!" Mr. Corrigan hugged me like a long-lost relative. "You're going to love the internship."

I got the job . . . ?

He introduced me around, told me to work hard, and then took me back to the personnel department, where they told me all the particulars of my new job. My first "real" job. I was a banker. Yeah, I had to start in the mailroom, but so what? I was having the time of my life: Peace at home, two jobs, and money in my pocket. And in 12 weeks, I would be in Atlanta for school. Who had it better than me? Nobody.

My first assignment was to sort and deliver internal mail. This gave me an opportunity to see all departments in the bank. I was energetic and cheerful, and I took each and every assignment very seriously. I got to know all of the department heads and received glowing reports. Every once in a while, Mr. Corrigan would pull me into his office for a quick chat, which I am sure some folks could not understand. My experience at Bank of Delaware is one of the main reasons why to this day, I treat every employee with respect and dignity. I treat the janitor the same way that I treat the president—not only because I was raised right, but because I remember how I was treated at Bank of Delaware

Then one day, it all came crashing down. I was called to the personnel department, where the human resources manager informed me that someone had been forging internal petty cash vouchers. My first thoughts were, *Why am I here? I have no idea who could do that. I have no access to checks. What is a petty cash voucher? And how do you forge one? I work in the mailroom. Do they think that I know who did it?* The head of security, who in no uncertain terms identified me as the culprit, soon joined us. One of the tellers had said that I was the one cashing the forged petty cash vouchers. The police were called and I was arrested, placed in handcuffs, and led out of the bank to a waiting police car.

Just like that, my world was turned upside down. No Morehouse, no future banker, no kid that made it out.

The cops couldn't have cared less. They said, "What's your name, boy?"

"Raymond Lambert," I said.

"Are you related to the Lamberts from Marshallton?"

"Yes, sir."

"Then we really know you did it," the cops said. "It will be a lot easier if you just fess up."

The cops' behavior was typical in trying to force a confession, but luckily my father had given me the talk early and often about how to act and respond to police. So I did not say a word other than, "Yes, sir," "No, sir," and "When can I make my phone call?" I had been in the jailhouse before—once as a 10-year-old with my mentor/self-appointed godfather Mr. Crawford, the bail bondsman, and several other times with my dad to bail my uncles out of jail, so I knew the drill. Also, by that time in my life, I had known numerous cats from the neighborhood who had been arrested and served time in jail. They would come back to the block and tell us all about it. They were often proud of it—it was like going away to college for them. I, on the other hand, never thought I would would ever see the inside of a cell myself.

I was booked and put in a holding cell—just another brother on lockdown. I asked again, "When do I get my one phone call?"

Their abrupt response was, "When we tell you."

"Thank you, sir."

While I was in there, another cat who worked at the bank was brought in. I'm like, "They got you, too?"

He said, "Yeah, they caught me. I did it."

"*What*?! Did you confess?"

He said he did.

I knew him from work, but we had never hung out. I sometimes saw him in the cafeteria, and that was about it. What struck me was that we looked nothing alike. He was dark-skinned; I was fair. He was 6'2" and 230 pounds. I was 5'9" and 135 pounds soaking wet.

I said, "Dude, please tell them again when they come back here."

"I will," he said.

After several hours, I got my one phone call and called my father. I lost it. Crying uncontrollably, I told him, "I'm in jail. They say I forged some petty cash vouchers."

"I know you're not that damn stupid! I am on my way," he replied.

Very shortly thereafter, my dad was there with a lawyer. He bailed me out, but despite the other guy's confession, the cops insisted we were co-conspirators. I was a month away from living out my dream of attending Morehouse College, and now I had a trial date for a crime I didn't commit. I had never been in trouble beyond staying out past curfew. I would never knowingly do something that could send me to jail. Our attorney was successful in getting us a speedy hearing, and it was set for two weeks prior to my departure for Morehouse. I told no one. I stayed in the house. Mr. Corrigan couldn't talk to me since it was a pending case. It was insane!

On the day of the hearing, my lawyer got a call on the steps of the courthouse. All charges were dropped. My record would be wiped clean as if this had never happened. Everyone was apologetic: "Big mistake . . . our bad." The bank paid me all of my back pay plus bonuses and offered me my job back in the program for the next summer.

My dad, though, was furious and wanted to sue, whatever the expense. The lawyer advised us not to. We were a working-class family with no status politically or socially. They'd fight us tooth and nail, drag it out, and all we would get was aggravation and an exorbitant legal bill.

"Just forget it," the lawyer told my dad and me. "Take your pay, come back and work at the bank next summer. Go get on that plane and get down to Morehouse College and make us all proud."

And that's exactly what I did.

Morehouse College made me the man that I am today.

I was following in the footsteps of cultural giants, but beyond that, my acceptance at Morehouse represented freedom. Like most young people going off to college, I was looking forward to being on my own for the first time. But more importantly, for me, attending Morehouse represented liberation from religious doctrine. There would be no more sparring with clerics about piety or debating classmates and constantly challenging their narrow perceptions of what a young black male was supposed to be. In the nurturing, all-black, all-male environment that is Morehouse, I was finally free to be in a comfortable place to grow and flourish.

Neither my parents nor I had any clue about the time-honored rite of passage of parents shepherding their young 'uns out of the nest and depositing them under a watchful eye in their campus dorm rooms. My father took the bus alone to the enlisting station when he enlisted in the army, so my taking a flight to college by myself seemed like a step up. I set off for Morehouse on my own. I waved goodbye to my mother, father, and brother at Philadelphia International Airport and, excitement twisting my insides, boarded a plane—my first—for Atlanta.

When I finally set foot on campus for the first time (I hadn't taken a pre-admission tour), I was taken aback by the lack of grandeur at the grand old institution. This was *Morehouse*, the breeding ground for so many of the best and brightest that my people had to offer? Aesthetically, it was nothing like the colleges and universities I had visited: Swarthmore, Lehigh, and the University of Delaware. Given Morehouse's reputation, I thought it would be a beautiful, bucolic campus. It was none of that. But the thing was, I didn't give a shit. It really didn't matter. I didn't care what the campus looked like, where I'd be living, if we had air-conditioning, or what they served for breakfast, lunch, or dinner. I would have camped in a tent on the campus parking lot with bread and water every day for all I cared. I did not give a fuck.

Rather than an African American version of the Ivy League, Morehouse is a no-frills, bare-bones operation—or at least it was when I was there. Instead of a cocoon where the children of the black glitterati are shielded from the slings and arrows of racism and insulated from the "real world" for four or more years, Morehouse is essentially a boot camp designed to challenge and bring out the best in its young recruits.

My first night on campus, I was awakened at 3 a.m. by a BOOM-BOOM knock at the door.

"Underclassmen, wake you up!" our RA bellowed. "You got five minutes to get dressed and meet us downstairs in the lobby, and we'll march you out to the center of campus."

Once we reached the center of campus, the staff read to us from the student handbook about what was expected of a Morehouse Man:

- "A Morehouse Man is *well read*: Read books, not just summaries of books. Books open doors and allow us to peek around the walls that society can sometimes build in front of us. Leaders must be well read."
- "A Morehouse Man is *well spoken*: Just as important as reading is the study of grammar and syntax. This reduces the necessity of relying on profanity or empty verbal placeholders like 'um,' 'uh,' 'ahh,' or nonsense like, 'You know what I'm saying?' Leaders mean what they say and they say what they mean."
- "A Morehouse Man is *well traveled*: Seeing the world outside of your own community opens your eyes to opportunities and the needs of others in much bigger and more meaningful ways than you could ever imagine from the comfort of 'home.' Get out there, break new ground, and take others with you. Leaders go . . . ."

- "A Morehouse Man is *well dressed:* The way you dress does not only reflect the way you feel about yourself, it also sends signals to the people around you. Morehouse doesn't have a strict dress code, but you can enjoy yourself while wearing comfortable clothing that respects the fact that you are part of a community of educated and ethical men. Wear what you wish to off-campus, but while you are here on the ground where Benjamin Mays and Martin Luther King Jr. and Maynard Jackson walked, you will be well dressed. The way you dress can be a direct reflection of your respect for others. Leaders present themselves in a respectful manner."
- "A Morehouse Man is *well balanced*: Being a strong leader is about attaining skills such as compassion, civility, integrity, and even listening well. Be spiritually disciplined, intellectually astute, morally wise, humble, and willing to lift others as they climb to new heights. Being well balanced prepares us for the unexpected and allows us the ability to act and react to the world in positive ways. Leaders are well balanced and well rounded."

This orientation in the center of campus was an incredibly moving event. It reminded me of a pregame speech that coaches give before the big game. But this was not about sports. This was about the game of life.

At the end of the indoctrination, the staff asked us to look up at the stars and told us, "It must be borne in mind that the tragedy of life doesn't lie in not reaching your goal. The tragedy lies in having no goal to reach. It isn't a calamity to die with dreams unfulfilled, but it is a calamity not to dream. It is not a disgrace not to reach the stars, but it is a disgrace to have no stars to reach for. Not failure, but low aim is sin." This quote was from Dr. Benjamin E. Mays, the president of Morehouse from 1940 to 1967. I was acutely aware of the high expectations placed on my fellow freshmen and me. I was living on the same floor where Martin Luther King had lived. I was all in.

At Morehouse, students weren't pampered or catered to but rather pushed to realize their full potential. I was disappointed to find that I was already behind and, according to my academic advisers, in need of remedial classes. For most of my life up until then, it had been simply not cool to be perceived as book-smart. At Morehouse, however, it was not only cool to be smart but also uncool to be ignorant. I did what I had to do. After the necessary remedial classes, and with my professors' guidance, I was soon on par with my classmates—and even ahead of them in some areas.

Not that my focus was strictly on academics. My work-study job was in the athletics department, where I ran the intramural basketball program, coached, and refereed. I also dabbled in student government (hated it), but the major extracurricular activity I participated in was pledging the Kappa Alpha Psi fraternity. I set my sights on becoming a Kappa with the tenacity that I had formerly applied to excelling on the basketball court.

The summer prior to the interview process, I handwrote every Kappa at Morehouse and nearby Clark College and told them why I wanted to be a Kappa. I'm talking about 35–45 people in the years before Microsoft Word. It took me a month to get every letter perfect. Pledging was very competitive. Fortunately, my persistence paid off. Of the 106 applicants to the fraternity during my pledge year, only 16 were picked, and I was one of only three pledges voted in unanimously.

Kappa stood for everything that I wanted: "Achievement in every field of human endeavor." My first basketball coach was a Kappa, my favorite middle school teacher was a Kappa, and two of my best friends from high school had gone on to pledge Kappa. It was just the best fraternity on the yard. I did not even bother to research any other organization. Why? I know when something is right for me. It just clicks.

When you hear the term "fraternity," the first things that may come to mind are scenes of drunken debauchery like those immortalized in *Animal House*. But in contrast to this party-animal image, African American fraternities are centered more on a sense of purpose, community involvement, and mutual support—brotherhood in the truest sense. They were founded because African Americans couldn't join white fraternities. Kappa was founded on January 5, 1911, on the campus of Indiana University. The original name was Kappa Alpha Nu, but when white students began to call it "Kappa Alpha Nigger," they changed it to Kappa Alpha Psi. The Pi Chapter at Morehouse was the first chapter that was founded in the Deep South.

In pledging, I had to endure rituals like those depicted in the 1988 film *School Daze*, which was directed by Spike Lee and featured Samuel L. Jackson—both Morehouse alumni. As if we were joining the military, new recruits had to prove our mettle and manhood by showing we were tough enough to take the hazing. Forced humiliation, degradation, and brutality are all part of the tradition of pledging a fraternity. It may sound barbaric, but this is the way the brothers determine whether you truly want it. The mantra was, "The ultimate measure of a man is not where he stands in moments of comfort and convenience but where he stands at times of challenge and controversy." I did not want, expect, or receive any special treatment, and I was a willing participant in everything I was subjected to. And at the time, I was very proud of that.

My time at Morehouse made an indelible impression on me. Despite the quality education that Morehouse and other Historically Black Colleges and Universities (HBCUs) offer, they are too often unfairly judged. I was determined not to be bound by the same misconceptions, held by both blacks and whites, that black-run organizations are inherently inferior. I understood completely my responsibility to be a positive contributor to society and my race. It was not a burden but an opportunity. I could not wait to get started. I carried the legacy of "The House" with me when James Alexander and I founded All Jokes Aside.

Despite the perception that earning a degree from an HBCU might stigmatize an African American who's just starting out, top companies wooed us soon-to-be Morehouse graduates. I had my pick of opportunities that would enable me to gain experience in my chosen field.

I'd developed an interest in brand management. As far as I could tell, it provided the best training for an aspiring entrepreneur, especially at a Fortune 500 company. With hard work and a little luck, you could literally be running a multimillion-dollar brand in short order. And what better place to hone my skills than the world's most famous brand? I accepted a job with the Coca-Cola Company—specifically, the foods division, which was based in Houston.

I was offered two openings—one in Los Angeles and the other in Omaha, Nebraska. Considering I later ventured into show business, it might seem perfectly logical that I would have naturally gravitated toward the entertainment capital of the world. At the time, though, I had no interest in the entertainment business, and my ultimate goal was to live in New York City. I've never really liked Los Angeles, and I've always been suspicious of conventional wisdom. So instead of heading west to LA, I packed my bags and headed for the rolling plains of Omaha.

I had a plan. There is no better way to learn a brand than in sales. It's a great way to advance into brand management. Thus, I figured the sales job in Omaha would equip me with valuable experience that I could draw on someday when I realized my goal of going into brand management and, ultimately, when I went into business for myself. Moreover, the Omaha division was one of the top-performing divisions in the company, and it was on the radar of the top brass. I was told, "Keep your mouth shut and your ears open, work hard, and you'll be promoted in two years."

It didn't take me long to adjust to life in Omaha, which was neither a small town nor a booming metropolis. Omaha was more than double the size of my hometown of Wilmington, which had about 100,000 people when I was growing up. The fact that several Morehouse alumni and Kappa fraternity brothers had already settled in Omaha helped smooth the transition. The first call I made was to the alumni chapters.

At Coca-Cola, I was a territory sales manager who managed 75 retail and wholesale grocery store accounts and was responsible for selling frozen and refrigerated goods such as Minute Maid, Five Alive, and Hi-C products to grocery stores. I sold merchandising concepts, obtained authorization for new items, and developed all local advertising. I made something like $45,000 in annual salary in today's dollars, plus I received full benefits, two weeks of vacation, and a company car. Add to that world-class sales training, a methodology I use to this very day. I loved my new job.

Though it was only my first year, I decided to aim for becoming one of the top five sales associates. The goal may have seemed overly ambitious for a recent college graduate who was still learning, but my manager at Coca-Cola, Curt Meir, indirectly enabled my aspirations. On my first day, he told me, "I'll be damned if I'm going to let a first-time person bring down the team. So whatever you need from me, you let me know, because we're going to be the top performing team in the region; my promotion depends on it."

I didn't have a problem with that. I immediately felt right at home. I had always been taught that they keep score for a reason. And I not only like winning, I expect to win. My manager's rallying call brought to mind when my basketball coaches challenged me to step up my game. Determined to rise to the challenge, I hustled my ass off. I would ensure I knew my products' features and benefits cold. I set my sights on knowing my competition and making fast friends with my customers. My single-minded focus included rearranging entire frozen-food sections at grocery stores to get a single new product in the freezer case. As Coca-Cola's representative, anytime the company wanted to introduce a new item, I was the one who literally placed it on the shelf. This gave me an opportunity to give each product the best placement.

When stocking new items, I'd start at midnight and work until 4 a.m., when the store was closed. I had to wear gloves to avoid the freezer burn. That helped, but it didn't always work. Freezer burn was part of the job, but putting up with it paid off. When Coca-Cola added up the sales numbers during my first year on the job, I was in the top five. I repeated the feat again my second year.

Being one of only two African Americans on a team of 25 also required me to draw on my experience of being in the minority at Salesianum. There were certain towns in Nebraska where they told me that, being black, I couldn't stay overnight if I valued my safety. I quickly learned where I could and could not tread. I was never treated badly to my face, and despite being from the East Coast and being a rare black face in that neck of the woods, I got along well with the locals. Most were working-class people just trying to make a living. I could certainly relate to that.

But conquering the territory that Coca-Cola assigned me was never my long-term goal. Moving up in such a large enterprise certainly offered its share of perks and relative job security. But I had no intention of settling down and becoming a company man who would retire with a pat on the back for devoting my life to the firm, as my father and grandfather had done. I knew that the only way I ever would be justly rewarded and in a position of leadership was if I created it for myself. My goal was to work four years, get some experience, earn a promotion, and go back to school.

My goals were hastened after I completed my second year at Coca-Cola. At my annual review, senior management informed me that despite my stellar sales performance in my first two years on the job, I was not going to be promoted. They felt that I did not have "it" yet and they did not think I was quite ready for middle management. I needed to keep working hard and give it more time. What was even more vexing was that a guy whom I had outperformed both years was in line to be promoted.

I had heard this conversation about being passed over for promotions my whole life. Every man in my family had stories about how they trained every manager they ever had. They served as a trusted adviser as these cats moved up and up and up the corporate ladder. In 35 years, my father never missed a day of work. He never took a sick day and didn't believe in vacation. He devoted his life to the company, and when he retired, he got a pat on the back and a gold-plated watch. Fuck that. My father earned a good living and was able to provide for his family, but he was never justly re-warded for his efforts, let alone promoted to a position of leadership—which is why he wanted me to get the best edu-cation possible, believing that would level the playing field.

So I was fully prepared for that "keep working hard and wait your turn" speech. I had proven that I was willing to work hard and do whatever it took, but I also wanted to be rewarded for my efforts. I wanted to rise as far and as high as my talents and abilities would take me. If Coca-Cola did not feel I was ready, so be it. In the words of Paulo Coelho, "It's better to lose some of the battles in the struggle for your dreams than to be defeated without ever knowing what you're fighting for."

I began to plan my exit—into an MBA program. In looking at business schools, I was drawn to the case method form of study. Working on real case studies—actual events that took place in the business arena—seemed more real-world to me than other methods. In my research, I found out that only two schools offered the case method: the Darden School of Business at the University of Virginia and Harvard Business School. I've never been one to shy away from taking a risk, but the Harvard mystique intimidated me, and I had that rare moment of self-doubt. Morehouse had a great record of sending folks to Ivy League schools, but I didn't believe I was Ivy League material. I'm the product of teenage parents, the first person in my family to go to college, just a cat from 28th Street. I didn't feel worthy of the Ivy League. In hindsight, I think that I would have been accepted and done very well. Several students I outperformed at Morehouse were accepted to and later graduated from Harvard Business School. But I was stuck in my own way of thinking, and I felt like my place was at a less-intimidating program, though Darden was perennially ranked among the top dozen business schools in the country.

There are three things that a top business school can give you: an excellent education, great contacts, and the benefit of its reputation. It's not like law school, where as long as you pass the bar, your academic credentials aren't questioned. It had been drilled into me since birth that my credentials must be unassailable.

When I finally arrived at Darden's Charlottesville campus that fall, I had some remedial work to do, just like when I got to Morehouse.

In B-school, there's a lot of quantitative analysis—if this, then that. When I got to Virginia, I really wasn't prepared, quantitatively. I had taken statistics classes and done well, but B-school quantitative analysis is a whole different ball game. Engineers did well. Marketing types like me . . . not so much. At Darden, they call people like me "poets." I'm pretty good with numbers, but in an accounting kind of way, not in an analytical kind of way. On top of the endless calculations, I had to prepare three business case studies each day and present them to my professors and classmates. It was an academic version of the TV show *Shark Tank*—everybody's goal was to at least appear to know what the fuck they were doing.

The case study method requires active participation. In fact, it represents 50 percent of your grade. So it's a no-holds-barred environment—very polite and dignified, but if you come in there spouting some bullshit, as my father used to say, they will tear you a new asshole. It was intensely competitive.

I soldiered on and eventually gained a grasp of the material with the help of professors such as Sherwood Frey and John Snook, who mentored me. There were only a handful of black students in the program, and Frey and Snook gave us pointers on how to acclimate and thrive.

Virginia is an old-money kind of place, and there's no question in my mind there was an old-money racial overtone to the place. There was one professor who didn't like me, and I knew it. He never called on me in class. But if my experience at Salesianum taught me anything, it was how to survive in a place where diversity wasn't the norm. I visited with this professor after class, asked questions, and made appointments to see him in his office. He was not going to be able to say that I wasn't working hard and that I showed no interest. Unlike today, at that time, there were no black professors at Darden, but despite the lack of diversity, I felt comfortable.

That's not to say I didn't enjoy challenging conventional thought every now and then. As at Salesianum, I was one to speak my mind. I was always reflective and respectful, but I had no problem offering a different perspective than most of my Darden classmates were used to hearing. One classmate from Mississippi came up to me one time after class and said, with no harsh intentions, "Raymond, you are not like the black people that I know."

"I know," I said. We both laughed—for different reasons, I'm sure.

In one of my case studies for an Organizational Studies class, my professor asked me to play the role of the husband in a case involving a young black woman, a Harvard Business School graduate who finished at the top of her class and had accepted a great job with a major Wall Street bank in New York City. Despite her credentials, she had been passed over for a promotion time and time again. In spite of her excellent performance, she was the only person in her training class not promoted. Finally, she confronted her manager and asked why she had not been promoted. She was informed that customers were not comfortable with a black person handling their money, no matter how smart she was. What should she do? I worked with another African American classmate, and we reenacted the case. I couldn't wait to get to class and explain my position: that the case illustrated why African Americans should circumvent "mainstream" institutions that exclude us from positions of power. If we had enough money to do it, which we did, we should start our own banks. We and we alone should decide our fates.

Some of my classmates said my position amounted to reverse discrimination. They thought I needed to be patient. These things don't happen overnight. I shared with them my personal experience and my family history and how I had heard these excuses my whole life. After that class, I got at least a dozen angry notes in my mailbox. After that, I felt like a little bit more of an outsider at Darden, and was avoided by certain folks both white *and* black. This was also the first time that I had witnessed the class system among white people. Among the people in my class, there was a clear distinction between old money, new money, and *no* money.

The next week, as it turned out, that same professor conducted a survey of the class by handing out a characterization of an MBA graduate and asking us to describe that person in as much detail as possible. Unbeknownst to us, one half of the class received a characterization that identified the MBA graduate as black. There were questions in the survey regarding where the person worked, what his title was, how much he earned, where he lived, what kind of car he drove, and so on. Not surprisingly, my classmates whose surveys characterized the MBA graduate as black saw him as working at a lower-tier firm, having a lower rank and title, making significantly less money, and living in a less-affluent neighborhood. They even said the black MBA likely had a cheaper car and less status in the community. I felt a sense of vindication. This survey proved that my perceptions about the fate of African Americans in Corporate America weren't off the mark.

Taking a stand and being unafraid to speak out ultimately paid off. My professor encouraged me, and his class turned out to be one of the best courses I took at Darden, resulting in one of the few As I earned there. I worked hard to maintain at least a 3.0 GPA to keep my scholarship. I was no stranger to hard work, of course, but Darden's rigorous course of study and the sheer volume of assignments challenged even the brightest business students. I had come to Darden fully intent on earning straight As, but after about a month, I went into survival mode. There was a saying among the "poets": "B– plus B– plus B– equals an MBA."

After completing my first year in B-school, I landed a summer internship that offered real-world experience in brand management. I dove into the cutthroat world of Madison Avenue advertising, and it was the best summer of my life. I was working in New York City, and I was making $350 a week, which was a lot of money to me at the time.

Having been placed in the internship through the American Association of Advertising Agencies, I was assigned to the Ted Bates advertising firm. I put all of my B-school,

Morehouse, Salesianum, and East 28th Street training to good use. I led a team that won an agency contest for designing a marketing plan to entice more students to participate in vocational education. I was named Summer Intern of the Year.

When I left Ted Bates, I had a number of job offers from top Madison Avenue advertising agencies. All I needed to do was keep a B average and a job was waiting for me after graduation. I returned to Darden fired up and ready to finish my MBA strong. But in my second year, the student body was even less diverse. A few of my good friends did not return. When I was attending Darden, the dropout rate for black students was 50 percent. In the general student population, the dropout rate was maybe 15 percent. Black students only made up 2 percent of the entire student population. I couldn't let myself be discouraged by the demographics. I worked extremely hard, stayed focused, and absorbed everything I could. I was also lucky enough to have a few generous classmates and professors who assisted me along the way.

Darden gave me an education that far exceeded my expectations. I am forever grateful for the experience. I feel incredibly competent in business from a practical standpoint because of the time I spent there. At Morehouse I learned the fundamentals, and at Darden I learned how to put the fundamentals into action.

Aside from formal education, I also learned the invaluable practice of networking. When I first enrolled at Darden, I didn't really know anything about networking. Just as at Salesianum, I didn't take full advantage of the symbiotic relationships I could have developed at Darden—and there were plenty to be made. Classmates with enviable pedigrees and powerful connections were in no short supply. In contrast to my working-class background, my Darden peers came from homes where their parents owned major-league sports franchises, national restaurant chains, and international banking enterprises.

You could say Darden gave me a crash course in the fine art of deal making. I quickly learned that deal making often takes place not in the boardroom but in social settings. A classmate would invite me to a party, and I would think it was going to be like a Morehouse party—there would be some honeys there, we would have some drinks. But at the buttoned-up functions at Darden, they had cocktails. *Cocktails? And what is that stuffy music?* I didn't even know what the people at the party were talking about. What they were talking about, I eventually realized, was how they were going to take over the world.

I may not have been plotting to take over the world, but as graduation neared, I definitely planned to find my place in it. The previous summer in New York, I had discovered that while I was pursuing my interest in brand management at an advertising firm, some of my friends working finance were making $1,000 a week—an amount that seemed like a fortune for a professional just starting out. So I turned my attention to getting a job on Wall Street. I started taking more finance classes.

Some of my African American peers figured that the best way to get around discrimination and get hired at a good company was to do everything possible to disguise their race when applying for jobs. But due to Darden's job-placement procedures—and my own beliefs—I never had the luxury of hiding my identity. At Darden, they made you put your picture on your résumé, which was fine with me. I'd rather have a potential employer know me before I even get there. That way, I know that they are interested in *me* because they've already seen me. Institutionalized racism aside, getting into a top Wall Street firm right out of business school is no easy task. Manhattan's high-stakes financial industry is fiercely competitive, to say the least.

I started interviewing with companies. Little did I know that most of those hiring decisions had already been made the previous summer. Many firms made offers to their summer interns, and very few offers were made after that. I also discovered that the class system was alive and well on Wall Street, where there were a few pedigreed, white-shoe firms. I've always been a scrappy kind of grinder, but no matter how much scrap and grind I had, I wasn't going to be working at any of those white-shoe firms that say, "You're not a good fit. Sorry, son."

I may not have had the blue-blood lineage to get on at some firms, but my tenacity—and good timing—played a hand in my success, as would be the case years later when I opened All Jokes Aside. E.F. Hutton was starting an entirely new division and needed plenty of new people. Because the division was new, it hadn't had interns the summer before. Other potential employees had already accepted job offers, so E.F. Hutton was dealing with what was left over—which was me.

Rather than working against me, having no experience worked in my favor when I interviewed at E.F. Hutton. They wanted someone with no direct industry background but solid sales experience—someone they could shape and mold into the person they wanted. They flew me to New York and I spent a couple of days there.

My fondest recollection of that time was my interview with one of the top bond traders on Wall Street. I walked into his office and he directed me to a seat. His first question was, "Who are you?" He held up my résumé and said, "Not this bullshit." He crumpled up my résumé and shot it like a basketball into the trash can. "Tell me who you *really* are."

I hit it off with this trader and the other E.F. Hutton brass I met during the interview process, and they offered me a job. I would be working as an associate in the global sales and trading department. I would specialize in fixed-income securities. My starting salary was about $115,000 in today's dollars, plus bonuses. I would be making significantly more money than my father, and I was just 26 years old. I showed my dad my E.F. Hutton offer letter and he could not believe it: "They are paying you how much? *You?* You can't even piss straight."

Getting on at a globally recognized Wall Street firm with no inside connections was a rare opportunity—especially as an African American male from a working-class background. Getting this break was apparently so curious that one of the black senior executives at E.F. Hutton pulled me aside one day and questioned me about how I got the job. This executive couldn't believe I was hired on my own merits and not through the stringpulling of a well-connected friend or relative.

As it turned out, I was a good fit. The late '80s financial industry was distinguished by bustling trading floors teeming with hungry brokers hawking the hottest stocks and bonds. When I walked onto the trading floor for the first time when it was fully active, I felt right at home.

Having been involved in team sports my whole life, stepping onto the trading floor at E.F. Hutton reminded me of sprinting onto the basketball court or running onto a football field. The fast pace and the risk of career-making rewards—or ego-deflating defeats—provided the same adrenaline rush. It felt very athletic to me. It felt very streetwise. I thought, *They are going to pay me to do this! Can you believe this shit?*

And the best part was, succeeding on Wall Street had a lot less to do with coming from a privileged background and more to do with knowing how to hustle. It was like my neighborhood, Salesianum, and Morehouse rolled up into one. It was completely different from the banker side of investment banking; on the trading floor, there were a lot of blue-collar, first-generation college guys—even some multimillion-dollar salesmen who never went to college.

As I soon found out, having an MBA wasn't necessarily an asset on the trading floor. If you had an MBA, it was assumed you weren't hungry; you were looked at as kind of a self-righteous prick. *Why aren't you upstairs with the bankers?* Fortunately, you can take a boy out of the neighborhood, but you can't take the neighborhood out of the boy. I was still street-smart. My instincts were good. I could still speak that language.

Wall Street may seem a world away from running a black comedy club in Chicago. But my experience at E.F. Hutton prepared me to become an entrepreneur. I developed a love for the capital markets. As part of my job, I studied thousands of businesses. I was part of the economic system, helping to raise money for entrepreneurs and firms so that they had the capital they needed to develop their businesses. It was around this time that I became aware of Reginald Lewis, the financier who led the group that bought Beatrice International Foods in August 1987 for $985 million. The buyout catapulted Lewis into being perhaps the most influential black businessman in America.

A native of Baltimore, 50 miles from where I grew up, Lewis attended Virginia State College, an HBCU, and earned his law degree from Harvard. And he was a Kappa. I met him at a fraternity dinner, where he shared stories about how he would be greeted by security guards and receptionists—"How may we help you?"—at companies that he now owned. They had no idea that a black man had purchased the company. What I remember most was his commentary on operating with dignity and integrity. Reginald Lewis was a god to me. He still is—more than 20 years after his untimely death in 1993 from brain cancer.

Just like on the basketball court at the Brown's Boys Club when I was a kid, I had to put in the sweat equity to make it on "The Street." I was making 200 cold calls a day, developing my book of clients. I felt very much at home. It was the best job I had ever had. I couldn't believe that they were paying me good money to do that—but I never lost the interest in being an entrepreneur.

While I made a name for myself at E.F. Hutton, I maintained connections with my Morehouse brothers. One of the classmates I stayed in touch with was another alum who had also ventured into high finance—my old friend James Alexander.

4

PHUNNY, GIFTED, AND BLACK

I like working for white people because they take excuses. You can call in sick: "I don't feel good today." "No problem; stay home, and get better." If you work for black people, ain't no excuse good enough: "My father died." "Mine did too, what time you coming in?"

—EARTHQUAKE

AT FIRST GLANCE, James Alexander and I might seem like unlikely friends and even unlikelier business partners.

James grew up solidly middle class. Whereas I was the first in my family to go to college, James is a third-generation college graduate. His father was a high school teacher and his mother was an elementary school principal. James's family has a long history with higher education, in general, and, in particular, African American fraternities and sororities. His paternal grandmother, Winona Cargile Alexander, was one of 22 founders of the esteemed African American sorority Delta Sigma Theta at Howard University. Mrs. Alexander and her Delta sorors founded the organization on the principles of community service and political activism. She graduated in 1914—six years before women gained the right to vote. After graduation, she was hired as a high school English teacher in Sedalia, Missouri. Mrs. Alexander then applied for and received a graduate fellowship to the New York School of Philanthropy, which since 1940 has been known as the Columbia University School of Social Work. She became the first black person admitted to the school's graduate program and earned a degree in social work in 1916. In another first, after graduation, she became the first black social worker hired by New York City and New York County. I was in awe of James's family history, especially his grandmother's accomplishments. But to James, she was just Grandma.

In spite of our class differences, James and I hit it off and became friends from the first day we arrived at Morehouse. We were both very interested in business and entrepreneurship and always felt like we wanted to start some kind of business together. Our first plan was to try real estate, specializing in foreclosed properties. We even took classes together before moving on to other ideas. While I pursued my sales position at Coca-Cola and went on to get my MBA from Darden, James went to work for Frito-Lay, then later earned an MBA from the Kellogg School of Management at Northwestern University. Kellogg boasts graduates such as Thomas J. Wilson, president and CEO of Allstate Insurance Company, and Roslyn M. Brock, chairman of the National Association for the Advancement of Colored People. Oprah Winfrey and her longtime companion, businessman Stedman Graham, taught a course there called Dynamics of Leadership in 1999.

Even though James and I were following similar paths, we had no way of knowing that after grad school, our professional lives would become intertwined. After the stock market crashed in 1987, E.F. Hutton was sold to Shearson Lehman, and in short order I was looking for another job in the industry. James told me about an opportunity in Chicago. Continental Illinois National Bank and Trust Company was starting a new bond division, and James recommended that I get in touch with Waite Rawls, a fellow Darden alum and a high-ranking executive with hiring power. I reached out to Waite, and he said he'd love to talk to me.

I had completed E.F. Hutton's fixed-income training program, and I was licensed to sell stocks, bonds, and derivatives. I had become a specialist in government securities, and that is exactly what Continental was seeking. I landed the job, packed my bags, and headed for the Windy City. James and I were back together again, working in the global sales and trading department at Continental.

With an estimated population of 2.8 million people at the time, Chicago was certainly a big city when I moved there—especially by Midwest standards. But from my perspective, having been in New York, Chicago had a much slower pace. I hated it. It was too quiet. I was used to the nonstop hustle and bustle of the Big Apple. I couldn't understand why I couldn't go to the pharmacy at 1 in the morning. Where *was* everybody? While there weren't exactly tumbleweeds rolling down Michigan Avenue, I didn't see much difference between Chicago and the plodding pace of Omaha. Sure there were more people, but it seemed to me that like people in many other Midwest cities, black Chicagoans had clung to a lot of the slow, southern ways of their people who had settled in the "big city" during the Great Migration.

I planned to make the most of the opportunity at Continental and gain more experience in the securities industry, but I definitely didn't see myself staying in Chicago on a long-term basis. I figured I would be there for a couple years and then get out of the Midwest. Besides, I never really felt comfortable too far west of the Hudson River.

After a little over a year on the job, I found myself at another crossroads when Continental decided to get out of the government bonds business. James specialized in corporate securities, so he was able to keep his job. Again, I was faced with finding an opportunity to build—or *re*build—my career.

Around the time that I was pondering my next move, I met legendary businessman Chris Gardner at a business function. A mutual friend, Adrienne Archia, who was an assistant to the mayor of Chicago, made the introduction. When I told Chris I wanted to keep working in the bonds industry, he said, "You should come see me. I want to get into that business."

As chronicled in his bestselling autobiography *The Pursuit of Happyness* and the subsequent blockbuster movie that earned Will Smith an Oscar nomination, Chris had overcome tremendous odds, including a homeless stint with his son, to become a successful stockbroker. Like me, Chris started out at E.F. Hutton—in his case, the San Francisco office. He made his way to Chicago in 1987 and established his own brokerage firm, Gardner Rich & Company.

Chris attributes his ability to build his enterprise to being in the right location.

"If you look at African Americans who've done extremely well in America, a disproportionate number of them made it happen in Chicago," Chris said in the interview he did for *Phunny Business*. "So wasn't nothing unusual about a young African American coming to Chicago with a vision and a dream."

Chris offered me not only a job but also an opportunity to develop an entire fixed income department and to eventually own a piece of the company. *Done.* I hit the ground running. Every day, I was the first to arrive and the last to leave. I knew this was going to be special. It was everything that I could have asked for. Chris said he remembers me in those days as "a very bright, ambitious, buttoned-down Morehouse man."

But he was quick to add with a laugh, "I wouldn't hire another brother from Morehouse right now if it was Martin Luther King!"

I'm not bashful about saying I was good at selling bonds. I became the top producer at Gardner Rich. But I never lost sight of my ultimate goal of going into business for myself. Gardner Rich was Chris's company, and as far as I could tell, it always would be. My thought was, maybe I could get something going independently and perhaps fold it into Gardner Rich. I had always been interested in managing the finances of professional athletes; that could complement the products and services that we were already offering at Gardner Rich. Or I could just start something fresh and created in my own image with a partner like James.

The comedy industry came onto my radar by chance when I returned to Atlanta to participate in a career day event at a middle school, where I talked to students about what I did for a living. An African American comedian named Rexx Garvin also happened to be speaking and we struck up a conversation. Rexx invited me to come out to a show, so I went that night to see him and he blew me away. As it turned out, a young Jamie Foxx appeared on the same bill. I told Rexx that if he was ever in Chicago, he should look me up. He told me, "They don't really book black comedians in Chicago."

I stayed in touch with Rexx, and he even proposed at one point that I help guide his career. He told me, "You know business. Maybe you could be my manager."

During my days at E.F. Hutton, I had developed a concept for a sports and entertainment management firm called Choice Management Group. I had printed up business cards and everything. My idea was that I would manage the business and financial affairs of athletes and entertainers. But I ultimately decided to wait, gain a bit more experience in the financial services industry, and then hang out my shingle. But to use a sports analogy, I was becoming much more suited to own a team than to be an agent or a manager.

I got another taste of the standup world during a business trip to Los Angeles. Since I was going to be there on a Monday night, Rexx suggested that I check out Budd Friedman's famous Improv comedy club. The show was called "Mo' Better Monday," a weekly showcase for African American comedians. It was a beautiful venue with great service, and the comedians were as funny as the ones that I had seen at the Comedy Act Theater in Atlanta. The Improv is also where I met D.L. Hughley for the first time. He invited me out to the Comedy Act Theater's LA club the next night, where many of the same comedians I saw at The Improv would be, including Damon Wayans, Martin Lawrence, Ricky Harris, T.K. Kirkland, and Robin Harris.

The Comedy Act Theater, which was founded in 1985 by the African American entrepreneur Michael Williams, was one of the nation's small handful of black-owned comedy clubs.

"I went around the country looking for black comedians and basically places where it was a showcase of black comedians, and I couldn't find any," Williams told TV One in 2014, appearing in the African American network's *Unsung Hollywood* documentary on Robin Harris. "It was all white comedians, one after another. And I said, 'Man, this would be great if this was all-black,' and that's when the light came on."

I had a similar epiphany, figuring that a venue showcasing the abundance of untapped African American comedic talent, within an A-rated facility with impeccable service, could thrive by targeting the long-underserved black market in the Midwest. If it could work in Chicago, it would work in Detroit; Cleveland; St. Louis; Washington, DC; Philadelphia; New York City; and many other cities around the country. At that time, The Improv had about 25 locations.

James saw the potential as well. He had also visited the Comedy Act Theater when Continental transferred him to LA for a one-year stint. James and I had been talking about doing business together since Morehouse; suddenly, this comedy thing really began to pique our interest. He eventually returned to the Chicago office, and during a trip to Atlanta for a homecoming celebration at Morehouse, we went together to see a show at the Comedy Act Theater's new

Atlanta location. There, Rexx Garvin was the house emcee, and Joe Torry was the headliner. This was a much bigger facility than the one in LA, more dressed up, and with a liquor license. You could tell they had invested a little more money in this facility. It was not at the same level as The Improv, but it was better than the site in LA and the original site in New York. The service was not stellar, but the comedy was. We attended both shows that night and had a great time. I remember that at one point, James and I looked at each other, and he said, "My God. There is a huge market for this." James and I compared notes. I said, "We should go to some of the mainstream clubs and see how they do it."

So we started going to clubs. *Lots* of clubs. The Improv, The Laugh Factory, and the Comedy Store in LA. Carolines, Dangerfield's, and the Comedy Cellar in New York City. I even went to The Comedy Club in Birmingham, Alabama. Unlike the typical comedy-club owner, Bruce Ayers, who ran that club, was legendary for staying on the cutting edge of what was happening in standup. He featured all of the top mainstream acts at the time: Tim Allen, Bill Maher, Rosie O'Donnell, Sinbad, and a host of others. I figured that if James and I were to venture into the comedy industry, we could make our venue stand out by drawing on our business backgrounds to create an upscale establishment committed to operational excellence. If we were to open such a venue, we would feature the best comics in the land and provide them with a stage in a first-rate atmosphere that would bear comparison with the finest theaters and restaurants in Chicago.

If we were going to do this, our concept would be to take the best talent available (the Comedy Act Theater), combine that with the high-quality operations of the top clubs in the nation, (The Improv and Carolines), and thus set a new standard in the black comedy-club marketplace.

James and I spent the next six months doing market research. We discovered that there were comedy clubs everywhere, locally and nationally, but we were at the tail end of a boom that had really exploded in the 1980s. Our foray into the comedy business came at a fortunate time.

There were more than 400 clubs across the United States by the mid '80s. An article in the *Los Angeles Times* put it best: "Everyone and their momma was opening up a club." Chicago was no different. All of the major national comedy-club chains were represented, including The Improv, The Laugh Factory, Catch a Rising Star, and The Funny Firm. While these clubs featured top headliners from around the nation, they rarely—if ever—showcased African American talent except for film or TV stars. Sure, there were nightclubs and coffee shops and mainstream clubs that occasionally allowed comedians to take the stage for "black nights," but prior to us opening All Jokes Aside, there was not one venue dedicated to comedy serving the black market.

Black comics would say things like, "White clubs won't give us an opportunity. There are no clubs that cater to us. You have to jump over pits of fire to get booked." Bernie Mac, the godfather of Chicago comedy, never headlined a mainstream club in his own hometown, and I would argue that he was angry about that until the day he died. If a comedian didn't have the crossover appeal of, say, Michael Winslow, who rose to fame for his ability to imitate sounds and was featured in the perennially popular *Police Academy* movies, then he was relegated to the "black nights" at clubs. It didn't matter how funny he was. It was not his market.

James and I saw an opening. There was a wealth of African American talent in Chicago and beyond, and we felt that the audience was there, given the demographics of Chicago. At the time, Chicago had over 1 million black people and a very strong black middle class. James and I sought to provide these comedians with a proper venue, to provide the audience with the best talent available, and to make money in the process. Win-win-win.

When we decided to open All Jokes Aside, neither of us had any experience running a comedy club or a nightclub—or any other kind of business, for that matter. What we did have was experience in the wholesale food business and financial services industry, as well as MBAs from top universities. James had also been a waiter in college, so that made us confident that we could make a go of it as comedy-club owners. How hard could it be, anyway? You need some comics and a spotlight, then you test the mic, open the door, let the starving audience in, and start printing money. Right?

All we had to do was take our business acumen and the skills we'd learned on Wall Street and apply them to an underserved market that happened to be comedy. Even though we had never done anything like this before, we thought, *Why not?* But first things first: we needed a name.

James often claims that he came up with the name All Jokes Aside. Let's just say that it is a point of friendly disagreement. What we do agree on is that I had a "Eureka!" moment during a conversation one day. I heard James use the expression, "All jokes aside," and I said, *"That's* the name." So in my mind, I named the club. But, of course, James sees it a little differently. To this day, he says he named it, and I say that I named it.

What matters is that the name stuck. Equipped with a name for our new business, we needed startup capital. There was no question that we would keep our day jobs to cover our initial startup expenses. We didn't even try to take out a bank loan for the business; working in finance, we were both well aware that banks don't loan money to people who actually need money. So both of us chipped in a personal investment. We each put $5,000 in cash and our credit cards on the table, and we were in the comedy business.

With that initial financing in place, All Jokes Aside needed a location. Rather than commit to a permanent location, we decided to rent space at an art gallery and turn it into a comedy club at night. I found that space one day when I was just walking by on my way to an independent movie theater that was directly across the street. It looked perfect. It was located at 819 South Wabash Avenue in the South Loop. The South Loop is located directly south of the financial district and is technically on the South Side. As I would discover later, it was on the Near South Side but on the South Side, nonetheless. The area was a bit edgy by Chicago standards, but it was rapidly gentrifying. There was a shortage of restaurants and shops, but it was centrally located and relatively clean.

The building itself was nondescript—a well-maintained, small office building with a street-level retail space that was being used as an art gallery. The gallery was rather large as galleries go, at about 3,000 square feet. The gallery featured paintings, illustrations, photographs, and some sculptures, all original works by local artists. There was very little foot traffic, so the gallery worked mostly by appointment only. They closed around 6 p.m. daily, so the space was idle after that. It even had a parking lot directly across the street.

Of course, I had no real point of reference. I had never been in a comedy club during the day, but my research had led me to shows in coffee shops and restaurants. So while the art gallery was not a "club," it was a wide-open space that looked to me like it could work. It was pretty. As it would turn out, not being a club gave it a unique aura. It was an art gallery that hosted great comedy shows. We surmised that all we would need were a stage, tables, chairs, a few lights, and a mic. We could rent those. And last but not least, it was only four blocks from my apartment. I could practically live there.

I made an appointment to meet the building manager, and James and I went in to make our pitch. The manager liked the idea. We were two clean-cut, well-educated guys in suits and ties who did not appear to be your typical club owners. What the hell? The space sat idle at nights anyway. There were few people living in the immediate area, and those who did were artists who occupied work/live lofts, so we would not be disturbing the peace. But the gallery owner needed to get the approval of the building owner. We came back the next day to meet with the owner, and he was just as enthusiastic. It would be a trial, a week-to-week lease can-cellable by either party with one week of notice. We could use the entire facility with no overhead but the weekly rent. We had to clean and pack up our equipment and furnishings each night and return the gallery to its original state. All for a mere $2,500 per week. *Done.* Based on our projections, we would make that easily. Or so we thought. We signed the lease and All Jokes Aside was born.

From the outset, James and I settled into a working arrangement in which James was essentially a silent partner while I acted as the hands-on manager of All Jokes's day-to-day operations. Like many business partnerships, James and I adopted roles that best suited each other. To help out with the business side, we brought in our friend Mary Lindsey. I had met Mary through a mutual friend. She, too, was in the securities business. She managed the office of a top trader and his group at the Chicago Board Options Exchange. She was a godsend because James and I realized we had absolutely no administrative skills whatsoever. She was well versed in all things administrative and, having to work with Type A traders all day, she knew how to manage difficult personalities, which I quickly discovered were not in short supply among comedians. Initially, she offered to help us pro bono, but as things heated up, we insisted on paying her something. We could not afford to pay her anything close to her worth, so we promised her a percentage of the "profits." She was game.

Now all we needed was a host, a house emcee. The house emcee was not typical in the mainstream clubs, but we had seen it work well at the Comedy Act Theater and during the various one-nighters we attended. Rexx Garvin, the comedian I had met in Atlanta, agreed to do the first series of shows but could not make a permanent move to Chicago. After all, we were not even open yet, let alone established. Not a single soul in the standup business knew who we were, black or white.

One day, I went to see this cat Bernie Mac do a midnight set at a local lounge called the Cotton Club, where he hosted and produced a popular variety show that included a live band, comedians, and dancers. He would later produce a similar show on HBO. The club was a predominantly black lounge in the South Loop that featured the best in black talent. Local and occasionally national acts would stop by and sit in. Cats like R. Kelly were regulars. When I went to see Bernie, he *killed*, receiving a raucous standing ovation. He was funny as hell and had a command of the show from start to finish. With the exception of maybe Robin Harris, Bernie was the best host I had ever seen.

I approached Bernie after the show and introduced myself, then told him how much I enjoyed the show. I told him that I was in the process of opening a comedy club and needed a host. Could we talk? He looked at me like, "Who the fuck are you? I have never seen you before. *You're* going to open a club?"

But he was gracious and the consummate professional. He said, "Sure. Come by Spices tomorrow night. I will be there with a group of the best comedians in the city. Show starts at 8 p.m."

Spices was a coffee bar in the River West area, another rapidly gentrifying neighborhood just north of the Chicago River, so at that time, they'd rent to anyone who could pay. Spices featured neo-soul-type acts, spoken-word poetry performances, and, on Sundays, comedy acts. When James and I went to the show, Bernie was hosting. Adele Givens,

George Willborn, Evan Lionel, Mr. Dos, Allen Edge, and a few other comics were there, and for the most part, it was good. I was already forming an opinion about what a show should look and feel like.

After the show, we let the comics know what we were planning to do and, despite their skepticism, they agreed to help. I asked Bernie for a sit-down and he agreed to have dinner with me to talk about our plans.

We went to a place called Moonraker that was across the street from my house. I hate driving, so I tend to go to places that are easily accessible by walking or public transportation. I had practiced and rehearsed the successful selling steps that I learned at Coca-Cola and was ready to make my pitch to Bernie to be our host. We got to dinner and it swiftly became apparent that Bernie hated the place. It was a "fancy" pub, and I realized I should have met him someplace like an established soul-food place on the South Side. But I never thought of it because I dislike driving so much. So we were off to a rough start.

I tried to salvage the occasion and made my pitch. "Bernie, we are going to create the best comedy club in America," I told him. "We will feature the best and the brightest talent both locally and nationally. We will be in a top-notch facility and we will have excellent service. In my opinion, no one has put all three of these components together—certainly, nobody featuring comedians of color. But we need a host, a familiar face that people can depend on. And you are the best. Let's build."

Bernie listened, attempted as best he could to enjoy the food, and thanked me for thinking of him. He said he was excited about what we were trying to do, but he was making his move. He had been at this comedy game for almost a decade and was ready to spread his wings on the road. He was only going to be in town maybe one weekend per month, and even then, if he got a gig at the last minute to headline at another club, he'd have to cancel on me and take the other gig. So he turned me down.

"But," he said, "I do have the guy you should hire. George Willborn."

At that time, Bernie and George were like brothers. I think Bernie saw George as the heir to his throne. I hired George Willborn.

From the jump, George assumed the role of the club's go-between with the community of comedians. The Ambassador. He became the fourth leg in the stool that was All Jokes Aside. What Mary Lindsey did for us administratively, George did for us comedically. George was that familiar face that audiences come to love, the one who gives them the assurance that regardless of what happens with the other performers, *he* will be funny. In fact, he was often funnier than 90 percent of the headliners. George would go on to become a national celebrity, and that rise started when he was host of All Jokes Aside.

We enlisted another local comedian and promoter, Mr. Dos, aka Fernandos Johnson, to assist us with outfitting the art gallery by day/comedy club by night. For the first six months, he rented us his audio system, set it up weekly, and served as deejay when he wasn't working. To get the club going, each night, we put together a makeshift stage with milk crates and a slab of plywood covered with a piece of fabric. It was neat and presentable, but this cobbled-together arrangement did not fool the comedians. It was regularly the butt of the comedians' jokes:

"Can't you afford a real stage?"

"You only got one stage light?"

"You call this a backdrop?"

We didn't realize this would be a problem; it looked decent to us. Sure, we had been in clubs, but our focus had been on the talent and the service, not the backdrop, stage, or lighting package. Most people have no clue what it takes to properly build a set and light it properly. It looks simple, but it's not. Besides, we could barely afford the space as it was. The comedians' teasing was all good-natured, but it did hurt at times because we simply did not have the resources for anything better. Not to mention that at bottom, we really had no idea what the fuck we were doing when it came to providing a real performance space.

James's sister Lori came to visit for the weekend after we'd been open for a few months. Lori was a seasoned veteran of the theater, and when she first saw our setup, she burst out laughing: "Are you *serious*?"

Lori was surprised that no one had been killed or injured by now. She and her boyfriend, Joey, who is now her husband, jumped right in and whipped us into shape. They spent all day one Friday calling every theatrical supply company in Chicago. By the end of the day, we had rented a stage, lights, and a real soundboard—thank God they gave us the first week for free. James and I were like, "Why didn't we know to do this?" We just didn't know.

We still didn't have a lighting board, so we would just leave the lights on. Lori and Joey would eventually show us how to create dramatic lighting without a lighting board. When it was time to start the show, Lori stood on one side of the stage with one plug, and Joey stood on the other side with his plug, and they kinda looked at each other, and then—one, two, three, go! James and I copied this technique, and for a year, that is how we started each show. We considered renting a lighting board, but the wiring to get it to work properly just was not worth the cost. A lighting board is also a rather permanent installation, and we literally packed up everything after each show. After all, this was still a test run. It was a good setup for what we were doing, and let's face it—we were not sure if this thing was going to fly. Not to mention that we could barely afford all of the other equipment that we were renting. Then I would go out onstage myself and announce, "Good evening, ladies and gentleman, and welcome to All Jokes Aside, America's progressive comedy showcase, where week in and week out, we bring you the absolute best in standup comedy. Where no two weeks are the same, and the customer is always right."

Despite these shortcomings, the talent was world class, and the service was impeccable. Moreover, the gallery's fine art was always on display, so when we dimmed the lights for seating, the room was beautiful. But most importantly, I felt, everybody *wanted* it to be a success—the comedians, the audience, and our family and friends—so a few missing lights and a somewhat rickety backdrop were minor. We were two young black men trying to bring something to the city and a community that was grossly underserved. We operated this way for a year before moving into our permanent space.

In addition to renting everything on down to the chairs our patrons sat on, like many first-time entrepreneurs, we began to find the bills piling up. The rent, the equipment, the furniture, and, lastly, the liquor license. In the city of Chicago, you cannot apply for a liquor license unless you have a lease. It is an arduous process that at that time took six months to a year. We did not have an official lease; we essentially had a handshake agreement, so we could not apply for a liquor license if we wanted to. Instead, we hired a caterer, strictly for the use of its liquor license. The caterer's license cost us $1,000 a week, excluding the supplies. We purchased the liquor and supplies and hired the staff. City officials started getting suspicious, since long-term occupants of a rented space used as an entertainment establishment are supposed to have a formal lease and an official liquor license. But whenever inspectors happened to show up during daytime hours, we had already stored the rented chairs away, and the space looked like nothing more than an art gallery. We were able to survive like that for the first four months. At the four-month mark, the city inspectors came at night. They told us we could no longer have a caterer's license and that we needed to apply for a liquor license. They also told us we could get an amusement license.

But even an amusement license costs money, and we were already hemorrhaging funds. How do you have a comedy club with no alcohol? We had no choice. We turned All Jokes into a sort of BYOB kind of a thing until we eventually moved to a permanent space. No one complained—not the customers, not the staff whose tips dropped by half, and not the comedians (although we did have a side stash for them). We just explained the situation and served sparkling water with the same enthusiasm that one would serve champagne.

We finally appealed to the art gallery owner to lower the rent, insisting we could no longer pay $2,500 a week and that the figure was exorbitant. He said, and I remember it like it was yesterday, "Raymond, I never apologize for making a profit, and neither should you. Let me see how I can work with you."

I thought, *Make a profit? I am getting my ass handed to me, motherfucker!* Of course, I didn't say those words exactly, but I made it clear that I thought we were taking it in the shorts. He threw us a bone and lowered the weekly rent by $500, with the understanding that if we decided to make a go of it, we would move to a permanent location in the building.

There wasn't anybody else in the South Loop that we knew of paying $10,000 per month for a similar space on a full-time basis—let alone to use it for weekends only. There was no walk-by traffic. We were a destination spot. Like most young, naïve entrepreneurs, we over-projected the revenue for the business and underestimated the expenses. Comedy-club financial data were not readily available; most clubs were privately held, so we had to extrapolate our projections from businesses like restaurants and concerts. We never asked, either, in part because we did not want to look like we did not know what the fuck we were doing. We were MBAs—from top schools, no less. But in business, you learn real quick that business schools are for developing managers, not entrepreneurs. Our business school training helped us tremendously 90 percent of the time, but there were other times when we just had to learn by trial and error. We were basically pissing in the wind with respect to budgeting and projecting. We thought in a city of more than a million black folks alone, the majority of them had to be over the drinking age of 21, and reaching them would be easy. Not so much.

Even with the rent discount, we were still going down the tubes—rent still late, checks bouncing, vendors crying foul. Since we paid the comedians (headliner, featured performer, and host) a total of about $2,000 per engagement to perform at All Jokes, we had to sell at least 600 tickets out of a possible 1,200 over the course of the weekend just to break even. *How hard could that be*, we thought at first. *Operating at 50 percent capacity?* At the first show, maybe 25 to 50 people showed up, and we knew all of them. But slowly, little by little, buzz began to spread. By the six-month mark, All Jokes began to attract, on average, up to 75 to 100 paying customers per show for two shows each on Friday and Saturday nights. But even with promising signs that the business was starting to take off, James and I had to reconsider our venture into show business.

When we first opened All Jokes, James's father gave us a stern talking-to about the foolhardiness of taking on such a high-risk endeavor. I recall James's dad saying, "You are 29 years old, working on Wall Street, making six-figure salaries, went to two of the top business schools in the world, and now you want to give that all up to run a comedy club?"

With the diminishing financial returns and constant strain of running a nighttime "side hustle" while working a full-time day job in the demanding securities industry, I was beginning to wonder if I should heed the warning of the older, wiser Mr. Alexander. Looking at the situation like a numbers guy with an MBA who was accustomed to evaluating potential deals on a risk/reward, cost/benefit analysis, keeping All Jokes Aside open didn't seem to be a winning proposition.

Simply put, the numbers on the spreadsheet weren't adding up. James and I began to realize that as much as we wanted to continue this thing, it wasn't making a lot of sense.

Enter Steve Harvey and the weekend that changed our destiny.

5

A PLACE OF OUR OWN

Please tip your servers; they are working hard for you tonight, and it keeps those sneaky bastards from stealing.

— GEORGE WILLBORN

EVEN IN ITS EARLY DAYS, All Jokes featured stars like Jamie Foxx, Bill Bellamy, Joe Torry, and Adele Givens. Bernie Mac, as promised, was a regular. But the success of that first show featuring Steve Harvey as the headliner in November 1991 convinced James and me that keeping the club going was worth our time, money, and effort.

We couldn't afford a hotel room for Jamie Foxx either, but when cats like Steve and Jamie were willing to sleep on the couch, and Bernie and Adele were willing to work for a reduced rate, we began to think, *We may be on to something.*

It was unintentional, but even my boss was helping out. Chris Gardner jokes that he was the original investor in All Jokes Aside—without knowing it. In the *Phunny Business* documentary, he commented, "Ray Lambert would be sitting at his desk crying because he was laughing so hard. I didn't know he was on the phone with Steve Harvey, D.L. Hughley, and Cedric the Entertainer while I was paying him."

Like James and me, Mary also kept her day job, which was with the Chicago Board Options Exchange. Mary assumed responsibility for all of the administrative duties involving the comedians, including making travel arrangements, issuing checks, and managing the day-to-day staff. She wasn't afraid to take on the role of enforcer. When the comedians or staff had an issue, she would handle it, telling them, "Don't bother Raymond. I got this."

The comedians had a love/hate relationship with Mary. They often made her a part of their act. Earthquake would often joke, "Mary was awful. I mean, she was harder on me than an ex-wife. I guess I look like the man that did her wrong." In all seriousness, Mary's no-nonsense management style was especially helpful when one of the male comedians had a gripe. Sometimes when it's a man-to-man conflict, we guys can't get beyond the alpha-male mindset. Mary was able to defuse situations, and she did it very well. She became that female voice that the comedians found easier to listen to.

Mary's ability to handle much of the day-to-day freed me up to concentrate on the time-consuming task of finding the best talent to feature onstage. It also gave me time to deal with the managers, agents, and lawyers. That part of the business can be interesting, but I would not necessarily call it fun. Most agents and managers saw it as their job to get the most out of me, the club owner, that they could. When they were good, they sought win-win deals, but this was rare.

All Jokes Aside continued to grow, and I eventually found myself at a career crossroads. Burning the candle at both ends began to wear me down—my days went from 5:00 a.m. at the gym, 7:00 a.m. sharp at Gardner Rich & Co., then arriving at All Jokes Aside by 5:30 p.m. I routinely got home at midnight during the week and at 2:00 a.m. on weekends. After a year of this, I decided to leave Chris Gardner's firm to focus on All Jokes full-time.

Initially, Chris didn't take it well at all when I told him I was leaving. He was very disappointed, and at the time, I couldn't understand why. It's not like I was starting a rival firm. Occasionally, he would come to All Jokes, and we wouldn't even acknowledge each other. Our egos wouldn't allow it. Years passed before Chris and I reconciled. But with the benefit of time and distance, I began to understand why Chris was so upset when I walked away from Gardner Rich. Just as I had a dream of launching a national comedy-club chain, Chris had long-term plans for his firm and had trusted me to help bring them to fruition. I was Chris's top salesman, and I generated a lot of money for both of us. He had a vision, and I was the guy that he felt could assist him in seeing it through.

I didn't make the decision lightly to resign my well-paying position at Gardner Rich. I enjoyed working for Chris. We were a good team. But something was missing. I realized I was at a pivotal moment. I could choose to continue to work for someone else or realize my dream of creating something of my own. At the time, I adhered to the philosophy that I observed working with great comedians: you can't be a great comedian *and* have a full-time job. You have to be all in. Not only passionate but obsessed. Even a job as good as the one I had. You have to choose.

Things were beginning to fall into place for All Jokes, but the rent was still an issue. We were paying twice the market rate. Our landlord did like us, and, more importantly, he respected us as ambitious, serious, and hard-working. So he developed a plan to keep us in the building.

In the back of 819 South Wabash Avenue was a docking area that he thought would work for us. He summoned his building manager and enlisted an architect to draw up a plan for a 300-seat venue. I worked closely with them and ultimately liked what they came up with. Customers would enter off of an alley, which gave it a very New York attitude. The set-up was very nice, and we would not have to make any changes other than directing our customers to the new entrance.

However, I could see early on that while the space was great, the landlord would not come off that $8,000-per-month rent rate, despite living in a market where rent for a comparable space was half that. The space did have the infrastructure, electrical, plumbing, heating, and cooling already in place, but even if we had to start from scratch and build out a raw space, we thought that we could do better. We still couldn't afford to take salaries but were breaking even by averaging about 150 people per show. I decided to take a look around the neighborhood as a way of demonstrating the actual market rate to our landlord. At the time, I had no intention of leaving his space. It was too convenient, and it was our home—the place where the dream began.

One day, on a walk around the area, I passed a building on South Wabash that I'd passed a thousand times before but just never noticed. It had an inconspicuous sign: "Commercial Space for Rent." The space had paper in the window, and I couldn't see inside. I knocked, but no one answered, so I took down the number to call later. I felt something about that space. It was one of those moments when you just know something is right. I looked at a few other spaces that day, but I couldn't wait to see the space at 1000 South Wabash. I called and set an appointment for the next day.

I knew as soon as I walked in the door: *This is it.*

It was a 5,000-square-foot raw loft space with requisite exposed brick wall. It was wide open, and we could shape it however we wanted. The building had once been home to a garage and then to a company that produced automobile springs and motor truck bodies. In the 1950s, American Wholesale Furniture called this address home, so it had a great showroom feel.

Despite my strong feelings, I went to our landlord and said, "Look, there are several spaces in the area at half of what you are charging. What's up?"

He hemmed and hawed, and negotiations dragged out for a month. Meanwhile, I stayed in touch with the developer at 1000 South Wabash, and he wanted us. He even came to a show and made us an offer we simply could not refuse. He would give us a "vanilla box" with all of the electrical, plumbing, heating, and cooling, 90 days to complete our interior design build-out, and three months' free rent. It was a good deal. We signed a letter of intent and began to look for an architect. Even then, we went back to our landlord. I told him once again that there were comparable spaces available for less, but he was convinced that his space was the best and that we would never risk uprooting our business.

Even though we had been discussing the possibility of taking the gallery space on a permanent basis, I had the sense that we were never going to get where we needed to be to make the rent. Our landlord had architectural renderings for the proposed new space, which we all loved. We'd have our own entrance and access to shared space in the building for storage and office space. We could have avoided the whole headache of moving. It would have been a cool space, and the landlord really tried to get us to sign on. But we had become a bit more knowledgeable about the marketplace and our needs. We decided once and for all to move. But we'd have to do it quietly. I liked our landlord, but I didn't trust him. He had "connections"—he knows who he knows—and in a city like Chicago, that could have been a problem. It might have meant he was in bed with the politicos and thus could make getting our licenses all but impossible. As my godfather used to say, "Business relationships are based on business—if there is no business, there is no relationship."

Finally, we signed a lease at 1000 South Wabash and hired an architect. For the next four months, we built in secret and acquired our licenses. No one but James, Mary, and I knew what we were doing. No other staff member or comedian knew, not even George Willborn. We felt that to execute it properly, we had to be stealthy.

When the time came to go, we moved out all of our furniture on a Thursday night so that our landlord and his staff would not notice. Then, one Friday afternoon after the building staff left for the day and before our staff was due to show up, we posted a sign in the door at 819 that said, "All Jokes Aside staff, please report to 1000 South Wabash."

The new space was awesome. When we finally took down all the scaffolding, pulled the protective paper off the tables and chairs, turned on the lights, pumped the music, and turned on the outdoor neon sign, I cried. It was everything that we had dreamed of when we started this journey more than a year before. We were not out of the woods financially—in fact, we had added more debt—but we were a real club with a permanent home. We had a venue as good, if not better, than any comedy-club venue in the country. A place of our own.

On the other hand, George and the rest of the staff were conflicted. They loved the space, but they were pissed that they hadn't been part of the process. They got over their disappointment real quick. About a week later, we had an official grand opening. The customers loved it. It was a real comedy club—24/7/365.

One of the tasks I devoted a lot of my attention to was making sure All Jokes was equipped with a well-trained, highly professional frontline staff. When we first started, family and friends were helping out on staff. When my hyper-attention-to-detail management style began to grate on them, they would remind me, "You do know that we are working for free, right?"

As we progressed, people in the audience would inquire about what we needed in terms of bartenders, servers, hosts, and security guards. So much of All Jokes's staff came through word of mouth and personal references. For the staff, I like to think it was a really good part-time job. And it was fun—getting to watch Jamie Foxx, Dave Chappelle, and Bernie Mac while you worked—but we never lost sight of the fact that we were a business.

Our initial uniforms were 100 percent cotton shirts and silk ties from a local boutique, Mario Uomo. I made a barter deal with the shop's owner, Bruce Gage. People would often ask the staff where they got their ties. The uniforms gave us a polished and professional look that was distinctive and memorable. Initially, I allowed people to launder their own shirts, but that shit didn't work out. Not everyone can iron a shirt properly. I began to provide laundry service to ensure the shirts were done right. The staff appreciated that. I wanted their clothes to be crisp and unassailable.

I also expected crisp service from everybody—from the front servers to the box office. In fact, our first box-office attendant was a homeless cat, Tony Dodge, who used to beg for change out in front of the club. He had a great presentation, and you could tell that he was educated and had good home training. One day when our box office attendant didn't show, I put him in the box office. He washed up in the bathroom, but his clothes were funky as hell. Even so, he was good. We agreed to pay him minimum wage on the days that he worked, and we provided him with a shirt and tie and laundry service. He got up to working four days a week—but he was an addict. He never stole from us, but there were too many days where he would just not show up. Sad.

When it came to training, I turned to the model set by Houston's restaurant, an upscale dining chain based in

Beverly Hills, California. Impressed with the service at Houston's Chicago location, I sought their advice. In my opinion—and over the decades, I have had the opportunity to study practically every major restaurant chain in America—Houston's at that time was the best. It was a national chain but with a mom-and-pop, local-yet-sophisticated feel. They ran a very tight ship—water would hit the table within five minutes of the guest being seated, and the first drink order would be out five minutes after that. If servers saw an empty plate or glass, they were instructed to take it off the table and offer another drink, whether it was in their section or not. Houston's philosophy was, "We are all here to serve the guest," but they made it look effortless and natural. They even had their own pens for the servers, and even those were the best pens in the business. *How much thought went into that?*, I wondered. God is in the details. They had uniformity and discipline in everything that they did. I loved that. I visited locations in Atlanta, DC, and LA to see if Chicago was an anomaly or if consistently delivering excellence was the way they did business. It was. I became a weekly regular at Houston's Chicago restaurant.

One day, I asked one of the servers I had come to admire if she would be interested in consulting and putting together a program for the All Jokes staff. She agreed and put together a stellar training program. I also asked friends who worked at top companies in the service industry if they would share their policy and procedure handbooks with me. I remember getting a small employee handbook from the Grand Hyatt hotel. It fit in a pants pocket so employees could study it during their downtime. I still have it. It detailed everything, including grooming standards for hair, fingernails, makeup, jewelry, and hosiery, as well as the proper way to wear a uniform. Getting it was like Christmas morning for me. All of this market research resulted in my developing the All Jokes Aside Handbook.

I worked extremely hard to overcome cultural barriers by providing the best training possible and creating an environment where expectations were clear. It has been my experience that, culturally speaking, black people often have a problem working for other black people, and we tend to have a problem serving each other. We can be incredibly hard on each other. My objective was to render both of those self-defeating behaviors moot. It wasn't easy.

George once confided in me that it created a great feeling of pride among the comics to have their own five-star club. The owners were black, the audience was black, the waiters and waitresses were black, the deejay was black. And they did not have to make any excuses for it. That was very important to the comedians. It was important to me as well. But we couldn't just take pride in being black. We sought excellence in all that we did.

At All Jokes, we not only had to overcome cultural differences, but we also had to compete with the mainstream comedy clubs to attract top talent. I fully intended to be the best comedy club in the business, *period*. By any means necessary.

And it wasn't easy. The Improv would do more bar revenue on a Saturday night than we'd do for the entire week. Enforcing a two-drink minimum was a chore.

Every day, every show, a customer would say, "How dare you tell me how many drinks to buy? I bought a ticket," or "These drinks are mighty expensive. I can get a liter of Absolut at the grocery store for the price of these drinks."

I'd say, "Well, how are the drinks? How's the service? By the way, who's headlining at the Piggly Wiggly this week?"

For a top-notch server, I had to pay two times what The Improv was paying. If other clubs were paying $2.50 an hour plus tips, I'd have to pay $5 an hour plus tips because so many black people don't tip. (That's one stereotype, I soon discovered, that's true.) I remember one particular incident involving a customer at the location we later opened in Detroit. This guy was a high roller and was buying drink after drink for the ladies at his table. We practically had to assign a single server just to his table. At the end of the night, his total was $200, and he tipped $5.

I had instructed the staff that when a particularly outrageous incident of bad tipping happened, instead of getting in a confrontation with the customer, to come get me. So I tactfully asked this high roller if there was a problem with the service he received, as indicated from the meager tip. He replied that he only tips $5, no matter how much he spends and regardless of the quality of the service.

I said, "Well, you do know, sir, the customary tip is 15 percent unless you're not happy with the service."

He still didn't seem to grasp what I was saying, so I told him what I told every customer who didn't think tipping was important: "In order to have great businesses within our community, we must support them. The comedians and overhead costs take the door money. In order to keep our doors open, we have to have a profitable bar business. All that being said, we're happy to have you, and no doubt, we need customers, but we don't need any one particular customer." I tipped the server $40 right in front of him, out of my own pocket.

I hope this incident illustrates the education process I undertook to show both customers and staff that "black" is not synonymous with "inferior." I've often found that running a black business requires a retraining process—you have to retrain the staff *and* the patrons to treat everyone the same way they'd like to be treated—the same way they'd treat their grandmother, their aunt, their mother.

In addition to implementing codes of conduct, I offered incentives and rewards for the staff and customers alike. I developed a bonus plan for staff that paid out nightly, quarterly, and annually, commensurate with the amount of sales they brought in. We had catered holiday parties and summer outings for the staff and their families. For the guests, we had a frequent guest program in the early '90s that offered incentives for repeat business. As I reflect on it, I feel we were quite progressive in that way.

I tried to come up with creative ways to boost drink sales, which is the lifeblood of any entertainment establishment. If we had a two-drink minimum, the third drink carried a commission—without encouraging overindulgence, of course, because if that person walked out of the club and got in a car accident, we were both going to jail.

Controlling the liquor supply was something I had to pay especially close attention to as the months went by. I "trusted" the people I hired, but I eventually became aware of fairly common practices in the entertainment and hospitality industries that involved employees skimming a little here and there.

I received some very good advice about cracking down on employee theft from Lillian Brown, the mother of my friend LaShaun and the longtime proprietor of several Chicago neighborhood bars. She took a look around All Jokes and asked me, "How often do you do inventory?"

I said, "Once a week."

"No wonder you're not making any money," she said. "They are stealing from you like there is no tomorrow. You gotta take inventory every night and in-between shows."

She came in and showed me the ropes on how to manage bartenders and servers. Keep an eye on everybody, she taught me. They don't teach that in B-school. You gotta learn that in the streets.

I took Ms. Brown's advice as a best practice, especially her suggestion to allow only one employee to have a key to the liquor cabinet so it was one person's fault if anything came up missing. I also implemented several other suggestions she had related to maximizing profits. For instance, a liter of liquor contains roughly 32 shots. I needed to make a profit off of at least 28 of those shots. This allowed servers to occasionally over-pour or to buy a friend a drink on the house. But if I didn't get 28 shots, the server would have to pay for the bottle—retail, not wholesale. Ms. Brown also showed me little things like how we had to put the drink prices on the table, because unbeknownst to me, servers were charging their own prices.

My consultation with Ms. Brown was like a crash course in the practical, day-to-day aspects of running a business. I learned to be more focused, such as in noticing that a server had placed a bottle of champagne on a friend's table and checking whether that friend had been charged for the luxury item. After I met with Ms. Brown, my sales immediately went up by 25 percent. That's the difference between showing a profit and taking a loss. But as I later learned, some employees were *still* stealing!

When All Jokes first opened, our ticket sales were affected by an employee who thought there was no harm in skimming a little of the profits. Early on, I began to notice something was awry when tickets for a given show sold out and there should have been 300 people in the club, but there were maybe 275 at the most.

As it turned out, the security guard was running his own operation by allowing his people to pay him cash under the table. Of course, the security guard had to go—after all, how "secure" could the place be if he was busier lining his pockets than doing his job? I don't know how much money I lost before I had to replace him. You lose some, you learn some. I hired someone else not only to manage the front door but also to monitor the immediate area surrounding the club's front entrance. Watching the front was especially important when customers were waiting in line to get in and an earlier show had just let out. If someone dropped a bottle, broken glass could turn into a lethal weapon if a fight broke out. Fortunately, such an incident never happened, but it's a business owner's job to exercise such vigilance.

To put it bluntly, despite diligence in managing, there's always the possibility of shit going off the ramps. I managed the outside as aggressively as I managed the inside. I had to look at every single aspect of my business to make sure it was running at an optimum. I would clean up the whole block at the end of a show.

Did the managers at Zanies or The Improv have to go to such lengths to ensure everything ran smoothly? Maybe, maybe not. Didn't matter. I had to. It's been my experience that black business owners have to pay what's commonly referred to as the "black tax"—taking extra precautions so as not to reinforce negative perceptions of black businesses being lax and disorganized. Trust me, the black business *will* get blamed if shit goes wrong two doors down.

My father's voice often echoed in my head: "You gotta work twice as hard for twice as long for half as much." I was not a fan of the "half as much" part. But I knew and accepted that for a black entrepreneur, the black tax is simply a cost of doing business. You gotta pay it.

While being vigilant was important, I also tried to be sympathetic to my employees' needs. In response to repeated requests for pay advances, I put my finance background to work and devised a way to help employees who found themselves in a bind every now and then. I got tired of employees asking, "Can I get $25 on my check? I'm about to get evicted."

So I put $2,500 in an account and called it the All Jokes Aside Bank. I then put together a "lending committee" of All Jokes employees, who functioned as an informal credit union, convening to decide whether to loan money when approached with hardship cases. If employees could convince the committee, the money was theirs. The committee members were 10 times harder than I would have been. They knew when someone was bullshitting. They knew when someone went to the club and drank away their rent money on Tuesday night. They knew when someone overspent on that new outfit. They could be understanding, but they could also be merciless. I could be tough when I needed to be, but I certainly wouldn't consider myself merciless.

When enforcing the club's policies, I strove to be even-handed. My sense of fairness extended to hiring All Jokes Aside's managers, John Andrews and Ben Ross, who are white.

Now how did I justify being a black business with white managers? Simple: I hired the best and brightest. I was an equal-opportunity employer. We did not attract many white applicants, but we had a few. They typically had come to a show, or they were from other comedy clubs and had heard about us from former staff that we had hired away from the mainstream clubs. John and Ben started out as bartenders who ascended to managers. They had extensive comedy club experience. They had worked at clubs their whole professional lives—places like Catch a Rising Star, The Improv, The Funny Firm—so they knew the business. Those two worked the hardest, showed up on time, did exactly what I asked them to do, and routinely went beyond the call of duty.

John came to work at All Jokes by answering a "help wanted" ad. His seven-year tenure at All Jokes kicked off with an auspicious start—Steve Harvey's week as a headliner was one of John's first weeks on the job.

John had been a bit surprised at all of the pre-show preparation for this guy Steve Harvey. He asked me, "Who is he? Everyone is so prepared."

I recall telling John, "You'll see. It's going to be busy. Actually, it's going to be over the top."

That Friday, the second-busiest day of the show week, there were three shows, 300 people per show, and more people trying to get in.

John helped Ben, who also had experience working at mainstream comedy clubs, get hired at All Jokes. Like John, Ben was amazed by the enthusiastic audience response for Steve.

Ben would come up to me between shows and say, "I've been around comedy a long time. Where are all these people coming from? This is amazing that they're all here. We're busy, but I've never heard of this guy."

And I'd wrap my arm around his shoulder and say, "Ben, black folk not only want to laugh—we need to!"

John and Ben both said one of the major differences they noticed between All Jokes and the mainstream clubs was that we had more of a corporate structure—and more structure in general. I like structure and reporting. I had an Excel spreadsheet for everything: ticket sales by show, day, week, and month. I looked at sales at the door, as well as start and end times for shows. I analyzed drink sales, merchandise sales, and bar inventory. I measured the effectiveness of all marketing and promotional campaigns. Before All Jokes, John and Ben had never been required to sit down and analyze data. It was my lifeblood. In fact, on any given day, I could be found with a spreadsheet in my pocket. I love numbers. Numbers may not tell the entire story, but they rarely lie.

John and Ben had all the tools to track the numbers. We had Mac computers, even back then, for them to use. I have always been a fan of Apple. That company did it better than anybody else, even then. But we had to have tech guys come in and work with John and Ben because they had never used a computer at a club.

I learned a lot from John and Ben about the business, and I was always fascinated by what it was like for them to be in the minority in a predominantly black environment. John and Ben said they remember race only occasionally being an issue—and even then, it was with customers, not the comedians, staff, or management. And the "race card" usually only got dealt when John or Ben stepped in to help a server when customers didn't want to pay up at the end of the night.

I supported John and Ben 110 percent. They busted their asses day in and day out. And they knew the business. Some customers didn't like it when I'd suggest they see Ben or John to resolve a bar issue. They would say, "What's this white boy doing running this club?" And I'd say, "We believe in hiring whoever is most qualified, regardless of race."

Running the club was fun, but make no mistake—like any other hospitality business, it was stressful and labor intensive. Hard work and stamina are prerequisites. As a staff person, the best we could hope for was to be present but not noticed. We had to constantly monitor and coach the staff. We assigned sections based on personalities—put the toughest server in the toughest section. Put a college graduate in the section having the college class reunion.

Even when we did well, customers could be brutal to the staff. To boost employee morale and show my appreciation for their efforts in reaching our goals, I would sponsor offsite get-togethers during holidays and special occasions. These get-togethers would often include employee talent shows at which the All Jokes staff would get their turn to be in the spotlight. One of my all-time favorite talent show moments was when John and Ben performed a comedy routine similar to David Letterman's "Top Ten." They ticked off the top 10 complaints they got from customers, and the No. 1 complaint was, "What's up with the white boy walking around like he running this shit?"

I see John often, and he always has a story about how a former customer walked up to him years later and said something like, "You were the manager at All Jokes Aside, weren't you? Those were the days!"

When it came to hiring, did I want to provide opportunities for the black community? Of course I did. In fact, it was not only a mission but also an obligation to do so. But when the shit hit the fan, I was less concerned with skin color and more focused on who could get the job done. I extended this equal opportunity philosophy to the comedians as well. I wanted All Jokes to be the place where if you were funny, could fill your timeslot, followed the rules, and appealed to our bosses—the audience—you could work.

6

A CAMELOT FOR
KINGS AND QUEENS

Men are so stupid . . . they don't know when they are in a relationship. I don't know about you ladies, but, fellas . . . . If you hit this twice, we GO together, we's a COUPLE NOW, boo.

—MELANIE COMARCHO

FOR BLACK COMEDIANS, All Jokes Aside was a place where they could be heard. For the comedian out there who was trying to work, All Jokes Aside was huge. They finally got a chance to tell their jokes in front of audiences who understood them best. I'm proud to say All Jokes Aside became known as "a Camelot for kings and queens of comedy." The late Roger Ebert coined this description of the club in his review of the *Phunny Business* documentary: "What Second City was for *Saturday Night Live*, a Chicago comedy club was for virtually every black comedian who emerged in the 1990s. All Jokes Aside was a black-owned enterprise that seemed to have infallible taste in talent, perhaps because it was the only club in the country that didn't relegate blacks to 'special nights' or 'Chocolate Sundays.'" Comedians still come up to me today and say that they only realized in retrospect what a one-of-a-kind place All Jokes was.

From the very beginning, I envisioned All Jokes as something more than just a "comedy club." I didn't see myself as in the club business; I was in the theater business. I always wished I would have called it the All Jokes Aside Comedy Theater because that's what we were doing: putting on a production. I didn't use that name because it was too close to that of the Comedy Act Theater. But I always acted as a producer, and I always did my best to ensure the stars of the show were well taken care of so that they could focus on their primary job—entertaining the audience.

In *Phunny Business*, George Willborn said it best: "We'd turn away a hundred people a night [from] a 300-seat club, and we did that consistently for years. That's no small feat. For me to be the kind of ringmaster, master of ceremonies, it was a great opportunity that I did not realize I had. But I didn't squander it, either, 'cause at that time, I'm still learning, still creating, still nurturing what ended up being some really genuine relationships with some really incredibly talented people, good people."

I worked hard to recruit the best comedians. The experience forced me to draw on everything I'd learned up to that point—business school, hanging with my Kappa brothers at Morehouse, even childhood experiences. When I was growing up, I used to sneak into the basement and listen to all my dad's comedy albums—Redd Foxx, Dick Gregory, Bill Cosby,

Richard Pryor, Moms Mabley. Ultimately, it all sort of came back to me.

In his book *Outliers,* Malcolm Gladwell popularized the theory that it takes about 10,000 hours to master a craft. It felt like I logged almost that many hours in the first year of running All Jokes. I threw myself into studying comedians' acts and figuring out how—and *if*—those acts would work at All Jokes. I began listening and questioning: *What was this comic's point of view? What made him or her different from everybody else? Did he or she have an act?* Mere joke telling would not get it done.

Chicago was a well-educated comedy market, and it always had been. Great comedians came from Chicago, and the audience was well trained when it came to appreciating great comedy. Comedians couldn't come through Chicago and be mediocre. So it was a great training ground for comedians who came from other places. Certain comics adapted to All Jokes Aside very naturally. It was a breeding ground for some great talents.

George Willborn acted as go-between with the comedians and myself. I felt it was necessary to have someone serve in this capacity, since I made it a point to be friendly but not to socialize with the comedians outside of work. My policy was that I didn't hang out with comics. There needed to be a clear line of distinction between work and play. Hanging out with them was a little like trying to be friends with your kids. Not a good practice.

I also had to work hard to overcome the negative perceptions that many of the comedians, understandably, had of club owners—a group infamous for paying late, paying partially or not at all, and failing to deliver on promises. Club owners—and rightfully so, I believe—were perceived as underhanded and grimy. In my personal experience, I have found that to be true in too many instances. I was intent on that not ever being the case with me. My mantra was to meet, if not consistently *exceed*, expectations at every point of contact that I had with the comedians.

One of the talent managers I worked with to book comedians was Bernie Young, an African American who went on to become a pioneering television producer. His credits include Emmy-winning talk shows like *The Rosie O'Donnell Show* and *The Martha Stewart Show*. As a talent manager in the '90s, his client roster included Don Ware and Shirley Hemphill of *What's Happening!!* fame.

I've stayed in touch with Bernie over the years. When I spoke with him recently, he told me more about why All Jokes made such a lasting impression on people in our industry.

"When you had a good operator, when you had a club owner who understood what he needed to do, that was rare," Bernie said. "And, on top of that, an African American who knew how to do it was rarer still."

I think it was an asset that I started out in the corporate world instead of the sometimes-shady nightlife business. I didn't consider myself a nightclub impresario. There is nothing wrong with that, but I fancied myself an entrepreneur who operated an entertainment enterprise. I wanted to run it like the Fortune 500 companies that I had worked for. I made sure the comedians and staff were paid on time, that all paperwork was in order, and that the behind-the-scenes operations ran smoothly.

When it came to scouting onstage talent, let me draw another sports analogy. In sports, you try to put the right team together—not always the most talented people, but the right cohesive mix of people who can work together best. Sometimes the most talented guy might not be a starter. It became a puzzle: How do I put these pieces together and put on a great show week after week?

I tried to think like a filmmaker casting a movie, and I sought out stars who would have chemistry. Comedy is performed in strict units of time. The typical show at All Jokes Aside had a house emcee, such as George, who opened the show with 10 minutes. Next up was the feature act, who would do 15 to 20 minutes. The emcee returned after the feature and did 5 to 10 additional minutes, depending on how the feature did. The emcee would go longer if the feature did not do well and shorter if the headliner was very strong and scheduled to do an hour. In most cases, the headliner would perform for 45 minutes to an hour.

I spent a lot of time deciphering how opposites might attract, as the old saying goes, and how comedians with different styles might create a yin-yang effect. In certain instances, though, it might be important that the styles be more similar. If I was going to do a show with Jonathan Slocumb, who was a clean, conscious comedian, I'd book a complementary act to keep the theme clean. I might not even use George, who was known for his blue humor, to host that particular show.

It could get considerably more layered. Like, *How do I mix a physical comedian with a joke teller? If I have a woman headliner, should I have a woman as the feature act before the headliner? Maybe, maybe not.* As it turned out, I often did all-female shows. I was proud when Laura Hayes said in the *Phunny Business* documentary that All Jokes Aside was the one club where she didn't feel sexism but rather that she was treated equally with the male comics.

Putting all the pieces together to make a killer show became my favorite part of the job, and I think I became arguably one of the best in the country at doing that. But a point that can't be argued is that audiences would see headliners and featured acts at All Jokes that they would never see on the same bill anywhere else. Ben Ross, who was a manager and bartender at All Jokes for nearly all of the club's run, said he remembers seeing some of the funniest comedians in the industry there. And having previously worked at big, mainstream clubs like The Improv, he wasn't easily impressed.

Ben and I were recently talking about this, and his take was that there are some guys you can set your watch by. Fifteen minutes into their set, they're saying the same punchline that they always do. But the comics that amaze us come back every set with more material and try new things. They are constantly evolving and improving.

Sheryl Underwood was very vocal about my showing favoritism to certain types of comedians. I have to admit that I favored comics who I believed were not only gifted comedians but who also shattered stereotypes of African American performers. Audiences who paid hard-earned money to buy tickets to shows at All Jokes were not going to see the same type of act week in and week out. Nor was I going to put a performer onstage who even remotely brought to mind a Stepin Fetchit persona. I'm a big fan of Lincoln Perry, the African American actor who portrayed this character in numerous movies and TV shows in the 1920s and '30s, but Stepin Fetchit . . . not so much.

The diversity among the comedians who appeared at All Jokes was representative of the diversity in the black community. I believe there's too prevalent a feeling outside the black community that all black people are alike. I thought the variety in our acts was another important thing that made All Jokes so cool.

One show, for example, I headlined Mike Epps with Andre Kelley, one of the first openly gay black comedians. Mike, who presents a very macho image, went on to become a movie star in such vehicles as the *Friday* series with rapper-turned-actor Ice Cube. Andre's delivery is vastly different from Mike's. Andre is very proper and well mannered. He's from a little town in Kansas, while Mike is from the streets of Indianapolis, lived in New York for a long time, and has a very urban vibe. If an audience coming to see Mike Epps discovered that I had scheduled Andre to appear before him, in the first three minutes, they would be thinking, "Who the fuck is this geek up here?" In five minutes, they would start chuckling. After seven minutes, Andre would have killed. He'd have taken them to a place where they never thought they could go or appreciate.

I thrived on shattering expectations. Andre wasn't the only comedian featured at All Jokes who didn't conform to society's narrow expectations of black males. Long before Laverne Cox became the first openly transgender person to receive an Emmy nomination for her work on the hit television series *Orange Is the New Black* in 2014, a transgender comedian who goes by the stage name Flame Monroe rocked the mic at All Jokes.

Flame is a Chicago native who was born a man but identifies as a woman. The audience may have initially been taken aback by her appearance, but she won them over with her self-assured delivery and big stage presence.

I remember one show were we had a heckler who began picking on Flame as soon as she hit the stage. I moved closer to the stage so that the audience member could see me because unlike a lot of club owners, I did not tolerate hecklers. When hecklers sounded off, I allowed comedians to hit back for a few minutes, but then I would shut it down. The show was on the stage, I believed, not in the audience, and hecklers could ruin a show for other customers as well as for the performers.

On this particular occasion, Flame signaled me to hold up for a few minutes, then proceeded to blaze the heckler: "Sir, what's wrong with you? Why are you fucking with me at work? I don't come down to your job and slap the dicks out of your mouth. I think you want me, don't you? Ladies, secure men are not threatened by me, are they?"

At this point, the audience was howling. She went on: "Sir, I don't want you. Look at you: you're ugly, you're fat, and my dick is bigger than yours. What can you do for me?"

Ouch. That heckler left.

Flame used to say, "I don't care if you put me onstage with Chris Rock or Adam Sandler. They might be the draw, but you will always remember the sissy in the dress."

Flame, who went on to write for BET's *Comic View*, prided herself on being able to hold her own onstage, and audiences were receptive—for the most part. I'd like to think that the professional tone I set at the club put everyone who entered on notice that all who entered were to be treated with respect. I booked unique comics like Flame, knowing that audiences were unlikely to see performers like her anywhere else, which would keep them coming back.

Another memorable pairing combined the aggressive, high-energy comedy of Steve Harvey with the more laid-back Deon Cole. Deon is somewhat like Steven Wright, the award-winning white comedian famous for his deadpan, snail-paced delivery. Wright might slow down the pace of the show almost to the point where viewers are uncomfortable. Since opening for Steve, Deon has also gone on to great success. Not the least of his accomplishments is becoming the first full-time black writer on *The Tonight Show* during Conan O'Brien's infamously brief stint from 2009 to 2010. Deon followed O'Brien to his TBS show *Conan* and, along with the rest of the writing staff, received Emmy nominations for his work. Deon can also be seen in a recurring role on the hit ABC sitcom *Blackish* starring Anthony Anderson and Tracee Ellis Ross.

But back in the day, performing at All Jokes was one of Deon's first professional gigs. Deon recently invited me to a taping of *Blackish*, and we talked about the money situation at All Jokes Aside.

"It was unlike anything I even fathomed. Like, me getting paid to do comedy was never nothing I looked for," Deon said. "It really wasn't until I started hearing other comedians talking about what kind of money they were getting, what they were doing, and I was like, 'Wow, this is crazy.' So, I still didn't think I was worthy of that."

Deon said receiving his first $700 check for performing at All Jokes made him feel like he'd arrived as a comedian.

"I thought I was the richest dude on the South Side of Chicago," he said. "And then I came back the next week and [was paid] another $700, and I was just like, 'Oh my God. I got a thousand dollars and $400 extra.' Like, I was like, blown away. I'd never had a thousand dollars at once."

Back then, Deon was like the polar opposite of Steve, who most certainly wasn't shy about demanding three times our standard rate of pay. And unlike the clean-as-a-whistle Steve, Deon had a laid-back fashion sense that matched his low-key stage persona. In fact, Deon didn't even own a suit. He ended up buying his first suit, at my insistence, before he opened for Steve. I told him, "You can't open for Steve; it ain't gon' look right. You can't wear Timberland boots and jeans."

At least for the first couple of years, All Jokes had a strict dress code. We were known as "The Motown of Comedy Clubs," in part because I believed in the Motown model of how to present talent in the best light. I set about putting the comics who appeared at All Jokes Aside through a finishing school similar to what acts like the Supremes and the Temptations went through at the behest of Motown mogul Berry Gordy. It's very hard to jump onstage for the first time and look sophisticated and graceful if you come straight out of the Brewster Projects of Detroit. It was the same at All Jokes with comedians like Deon who I thought could use a little wardrobe upgrade.

For someone with Deon's slacker sensibilities, wearing a suit was a foreign concept. But if he had to adopt a more polished appearance to open for Steve, then that's what he would do. So, being Deon, he went to the flea market and grabbed the first suit coat he saw. In his words, he looked like a hot-ass mess. But Deon didn't care. He was neat, but he did look very uncomfortable. He wore the same outfit for all seven shows of that particular weekend stand. And nobody said nothing. Nobody ever told him that he looked like a hot-ass mess, including me. He rocked the house and made for a perfect match with Steve.

Deon did say that after that weekend, the comedians told him, "Dude, that was horrible, what you had on." But he could now put opening for Steve Harvey on his résumé.

Dress code aside, many of the comedians brought their outrageous day-to-day personalities onto the stage. They were just the funniest people I've ever known, and working with them was great. You know the stars, the household names, but there were also the lesser-known cats like Rodney Winfield, T.K. Kirkland, T.P. Hearn—really funny, and great characters.

But there's something about watching performers early in their careers before they become celebrities. I watched future stars like Craig Robinson grow and develop when they were working their way up. Now Craig's in blockbuster movies and has his own TV show. It's remarkable to remember when guys like that were working hard just to put together a good 10 minutes of material. They just worked and worked and worked on it. Now we're all benefiting from those years of effort. Guys like JB Smoove, who went on to fame in movies and television shows like Larry David's HBO sitcom *Curb Your Enthusiasm*, were the same onstage as off. Many comics were even funnier offstage. But some were surprisingly reserved when they weren't in the limelight.

Chris Rock, he was just an awesome performer, even very early in his career. I outbid everyone in the city to book him, including The Improv, where he had typically performed before All Jokes started. But Chris was either on or off. If he was onstage, he was a completely different guy from when he was offstage. When the mic goes on, he goes crazy. But before shows, when we would take him to do radio interviews, he would barely say a word on the ride to the station.

Eventually, Chris and I did hang out several times—he was the one with whom I broke my own rule about socializing with comics. Chris was who I would've liked to be if I were a comedian. We read the same papers and the same books, and we had similar perspectives on many aspects of life. Hanging with Chris, for me, was like going to the neighborhood barbershop, in terms of our talking, debating, and philosophizing about a variety of topics. But as brash and outspoken as Chris was onstage, offstage he was quiet, reflective—pensive, even.

This came as a shock to the staff, who were used to the over-the-top image Chris presented 99 percent of the time he was performing. Chris was just one of those performers who has an onstage persona and an offstage persona. And I ensured that nobody bothered him when he needed time alone. I appreciated that he sold out shows faster than anybody else we ever booked. And he's a true comedy genius—he brought the house down each and every show that he performed at All Jokes Aside.

One comedian who definitely has a powerhouse persona onstage is Joe Torry. On one memorable occasion, Joe got into such a groove onstage that he decided to ignore my time cues.

In a comedy club, everything is based on managing time— seating customers before every show, organizing three comedy acts per show, and scheduling three shows per night. If one comedian went over his allotted time, the whole night could be ruined. To make sure shows ran smoothly, I would flash a light to let the comedians know they had 10 minutes left. I would flash another light at five minutes, followed by a signal to wrap it up.

Well, Joe decided to ignore me and keep going. Now, this happened during a Chicago winter, and people were waiting outside for the next show. People were going to be mad—not mad at Joe, mad at *me*. How would they punish me? By not buying drinks and by not tipping their servers. I continued to shine the light, trying to get Joe to wrap it up. But Joe boldly asked the audience if they wanted more and, egged on by their enthusiastic response, kept going.

Joe, as it turned out, is a member of the Omega Psi Phi fraternity and we Kappa Alpha Psis have a "friendly" rivalry with them. The audience was full of his frat brothers and their supporters. This made me even angrier.

When Joe had gone over 15 minutes, I turned on the lights in the club. He kept going, past 30 minutes. The audience was still with him. When he had gone over by an astounding 40 minutes, I finally put an end to the standoff by cutting off the microphone.

When Joe came offstage, I was right there, ranting, "What the fuck was that?" Joe was not happy with me getting in his face. He probably could kick my ass in a fistfight. But fuck that—it wouldn't have been the first time I got my ass kicked. And he was dead wrong, and he knew it. Besides, we always had off-duty cops in the audience (we were around the corner from a police station, and many of the officers were fans), and I knew they would step up should some real shit jump off. I was so pissed that for a moment, I forgot where I was. Joe eventually apologized and I explained, "You killin' me and what I'm trying to do here. You must respect the light."

After that, I instituted what we called the Joe Torry Rule. From that day on, I told the comedians, "Every minute you go over will cost you $100. You can stay up there the whole night, but you're going to be working for free." With every new contract I offered to performers, I began issuing a list of "Comedian Expectations": be funny, be respectful of the club and the audience, be on time, and respect the light.

Being on time: that was a big issue. I didn't tolerate tardiness. Anyone late for a show would have his or her pay docked and might not work the next weekend. Chronic lateness isn't just a "black thing"; it happens at mainstream comedy clubs as well (as does poor tipping, of course). But later for that. If I could get there on time, so could they. Of course, some comics always tried to bend the rules. It would be 15 minutes to show time, and where was George Willborn? Where's Mike Bonner? Where's Tony Roberts? My feeling was, this is your job, and the club is a place of business, so act like it. Some cats were notorious for being late. I didn't book them.

Maybe because of our house rules, most of the comedians didn't indulge in more serious vices when they were working. I never witnessed—and wouldn't have allowed—serious drug use or heavy drinking. I will be the first to say that I was not naïve, but I honestly didn't see it. If it happened, they did a masterful job of keeping that from me. We had a back door that led to an alley. Some of the performers pushed the boundaries. There were times when you could tell somebody had been smoking marijuana back there. Those times were few and far between.

I do recall some of the comics acting high, but it never really clicked that they were *actually* high. Honest John was the best at it. Deon Cole, I later learned, would go onstage high, and he needed something to help him remember his routines. He picked up a notebook—a prop that eventually became a centerpiece of his act.

"I went onstage and I was high as a kite, and I'm sitting and I'm reading my jokes, and I'm going, and people laughing," Deon told me years later. "I'm like, 'Cool.' And I check it and I do the next one, and cool! I was like, 'Good night!'"

When Deon reviewed his performance at the end of his set, he realized he needed to make some changes in the way he approached his work.

"I went and got some water, and I was like, 'Man, I can't be smoking before my show no more,'" he said. "And dudes was coming up to me like, 'That was genius.' And I go, 'What?' They was like, 'Dude, you was using your notepad, that was hilarious. Is that your new thing, man?' I was like, 'No, I couldn't remember my stuff 'cause I got high.' And they was like, 'That's your new thing now!'"

Despite the enthusiastic response to the notebook, Deon wasn't convinced that using it as a crutch onstage was a good idea. So the next week, he went onstage at All Jokes without it.

"I didn't do all that good," he said. "I pulled out the notepad, and ever since, it's just been part of the show."

Most of the comedians who performed at All Jokes were on their best behavior, but there was one very scary incident involving T.K. Kirkland. Having once opened for notorious gangsta rap group NWA, T.K. has a distinctively "urban" style of comedy. But appearing at All Jokes helped him reach a much broader fan base. One day when T.K. wasn't performing, the law came looking for him. I had no idea why there would be a federal manhunt for a standup comedian. And I'm glad I never found out.

"I'll never forget when the FBI showed up looking for him. We actually had federal agents in the club looking for him," Ben Ross told me. "When he came to town, his shows attracted a variety of different people."

T.K. hung out with some brothers from the streets. Who knows what they were into? The FBI agents did tell me after the show that if they hadn't been fans of All Jokes Aside, they would have come in during his set and taken him off stage.

Another area that eventually needed reform was how I evaluated the talent. At the end of the day, I couldn't make a comic funny. It was my job to find comics I thought were funny, but ultimately, we all had to please our boss—the audience. To evaluate how the audience responded to the comedians, I passed out scorecards to rate the acts from 0 to 5, with 5 being "Excellent" and 0 being "I would not see this comedian again." The reason I did this is because I got tired of cats saying to me, "Dude, I was killing out there." *Really? Let's see what the cards say.*

One guy who received a surprisingly low score was Dave Chappelle. Despite the fact that he went on to become a superstar with his self-titled Comedy Central show, when he first played All Jokes in 1994, he struggled. At the time, he hadn't been in front of mostly black audiences in a while, and instead was doing more mainstream clubs. He had settled into a standard routine that he assumed would work anywhere.

Twenty minutes into Dave's 45-minute set, the audience's reception was chilly, to say the least. Every comedian bombs at some point, no matter how good they are. And good comedians are frequently testing new material, which can be hit or miss by its nature. Like the rest of us, even the best comedian has a bad day from time to time. And Dave was having a very bad day. His cerebral material just didn't seem to translate. The template for many black audiences was Harlem's legendary Apollo, where they would definitely let you know—at high volume—if they liked you or not. We controlled that kind of response, though. We didn't allow heckling, as I've noted, and we tried to discourage booing.

But I could clearly see Dave's set wasn't working. He had 20 minutes to go, but something had to be done. People were getting restless. So I told George Willborn, basically, "Give him an assist." So very subtly, I gave Dave the light at 20 minutes. He came right off. George stepped in and gracefully closed the show.

George remembers the incident like this: "Let me just say this about Dave Chappelle: I think he's an incredibly, obviously, talented cat. I didn't get a chance to have as close a relationship with him as I have with some of the comics that came through All Jokes Aside, and I think he only came through once, maybe twice, at most, during that eight-year span. During that time, Dave was a much better writer than he was a standup comedian, in my opinion."

After that disastrous first show at All Jokes, Dave seemed to realize he hadn't delivered, and at the time, I think he feared I would try to cut his pay in half. If I was that kind of club owner, I might have considered it, but I didn't want to be that kind of club owner. I knew how talented Dave was. I liked Dave, and I agreed to pay him his full fee despite his abbreviated set.

Because I paid Dave what I'd promised, I was able to maintain a good working relationship with him. I later booked him two more times, but both of those engagements were as part of comedy festivals I organized, where he only had to do 25 minutes onstage. And Dave, for his part, clearly decided to do the best 25 minutes he could. He's a perfectionist and a hard worker.

Mark Curry, star of the popular '90s ABC sitcom *Hangin' with Mr. Cooper*, had a similar experience his first time at All Jokes. Some cats become stars on TV or in movies before their standup is strong. I personally think Mark Curry is a far better comic today, and that has nothing to do with his talent, per se, but rather with the way he's developed his stage timing. Today, he's a standup comedian; in the '90s, he was more of a sitcom star.

At All Jokes, we showcased a wide range of talent, from African American comedians with mainstream crossover appeal, like Mark and Dave, to comedians of different races, like Carlos Mencia, who's Honduran. I recognized early on that the Latino market was maybe even more underserved than the black market.

When I interviewed Carlos for *Phunny Business,* one of the things that resonated with me was when he said that performing at All Jokes was a career-defining experience. Not only was it the first African American comedy club he had worked but it was also the first venue that helped him realize that humor transcends cultural boundaries. If you're funny, you're funny.

Carlos would bring a few cats along to open for him, and there were a few local Latino comics that he nurtured. But what always made me feel good was when he'd say that All Jokes was different because we featured comedians who were trying to go beyond just being black or "ethnic."

"It was a place for me to go and realize that I'm funny, period," Carlos said. "It was a place where I could just go and be funny and not have to worry about this or that, or white or black."

Describing how he felt at the end of a show at All Jokes, Carlos said, "Wow. My material's good. My material works with everybody!"

All Jokes even had its share of white comedians, such as Snow Cone and Barry Sobel. Honest John was a regular and had one of the strongest followings of any comedian who appeared at All Jokes Aside.

Before long, All Jokes was able to establish a national reputation for cultivating talent, and the club became a pipeline for televised standup shows that reached audiences across America. HBO's *Def Comedy Jam* and BET's *Comic View* would consult with me all the time. I probably could have been a manager, but I learned I don't really have enough of a nurturing personality—at least not when it comes to catering to the whims of artists.

For example, there was one time when Steve Harvey demanded snack-size Snickers bars for his dressing room. I didn't know Snickers came in four sizes—king size, regular, fun size, and snack size. The staff brought him fun size.

Steve was livid. I pleaded with him, "Please, can you just do this show tonight, and we'll fix it tomorrow?"

At his core, Steve is a very reasonable person and we got along very well. But comedians in general, I came to believe, are emotionally needy people, and that neediness gets more intense the bigger and more successful they become.

Despite these kinds of demands, Steve *always* brought it when he went onstage. Some of the best shows at All Jokes brought him together with the likes of Bernie Mac, D.L. Hughley, and Cedric the Entertainer. This lineup later gained fame through their national "Kings of Comedy" tour, which was turned into a hit movie by Spike Lee in 2000.

I had been putting four headliners in a show together for probably four years before that movie came out. I had the Kings first. The Queens too. The "Kings and Queens of Comedy" tours, featuring comedians for whom I had provided crucial early exposure (and paychecks) almost a decade earlier, signaled changes in the comedy industry. Headliners who were able to make a name for themselves on the national scene began to play large theaters. Smaller venues like ours couldn't sell enough tickets to meet the increasingly large fees that big-name acts began to command.

I didn't have the vision that "Kings of Comedy" producer Walter Latham and *Def Comedy Jam* founder Russell Simmons had. They were both experienced tour promoters, and I was a club guy. My thinking at the time was, *Who would go to an arena to see a comedy show, anyway?* I had become a purist, and I didn't consider the larger venues to be the kind of place to see a comedian.

In my opinion, standup comedy is the most difficult of all the performance arts in entertainment. It is best performed and seen in a venue where the performer can see the last person in the last row and that person can see the comedian's eyeballs, facial expressions, and sweat. That is when standup is magical and presented in its purest form, and in its purest form, standup can *only* happen in a club.

7

I HOPE I'M FUNNY

White audiences applaud effort; black folk don't give a damn about effort.

—ARIES SPEARS

AT ALL JOKES ASIDE, we had a code of conduct not only for the comedians and the staff but also for the audience. I insisted that the customers conduct themselves in a certain fashion in order to do business with us. It was a two-way street—mutual respect. It was a top priority of mine to maintain a professional atmosphere so that top comedians would keep coming back. When they were onstage, I ensured there were as few distractions as possible, down to the minutest detail.

For instance, I instituted a policy that all food, drinks, and checks had to be off customers' tables before the last 20 minutes of a headliner's set. I didn't want people fooling around with the check while the comedians were getting to the closing part of their act. I gave the headliner that last 20 minutes to have the audience's undivided attention. However, one distraction I still laugh about involved customers refusing to give us their empty cups and sucking on their ice. Taking ice away from people was like taking a pacifier away from a baby!

My philosophy regarding customer service—as I told that notably poor tipper in the club's early days—was that while we needed customers, we didn't need any one particular customer. If you were in our club, I was going to give you everything you could ever want—and more than you ever expected—but you would have to dress appropriately and behave accordingly. I wanted to communicate to the customers that I saw them as partners in building something together that we could all be proud of. I was willing to do my part, and if they were going to come into my place of business, I insisted that they do their part as well.

The dress code at All Jokes, both for the talent and the audience, was one of the things that I believe really set us apart.

I wanted the black comedians appearing at All Jokes to realize that this was not a chitlin-circuit type of thing. I wanted them to appreciate our efforts to run the business in a dignified fashion that would always result in everyone being treated professionally. We were operating, I thought, at a high level—not *despite* being black but *because* we were black. This was a basic concept that informed everything I was trying to do at All Jokes. I expected the performers to show respect for the audience by dressing the part. Be well groomed. The audience, in turn, was required to respond in kind, and the audience rose to that standard.

At the height of our popularity, 1993 through 1996, walking into All Jokes on any given evening was like visiting an African American megachurch on a Sunday morning. The club brought together many different aspects of the community, from the bougie upper-middle class in their buttoned-down, understated business attire to the working class in their flashy Don "Magic" Juan–style outfits. (Comedian Lavell Crawford said it best: "You in Chi-Town. This is where the brother matches his green gators with his green suit.")

On many a night, it became a fashion show, whether you were in the audience or onstage. You had to show up on point. When a comedian came into a club and looked out into the audience and saw everybody dressed up, it sort of made that comedian feel like he needed to raise his game.

Carlos Mencia shared his impression of the All Jokes audience in *Phunny Business*.

"I mean, I remember walking through the line going, 'Damn, I better be really funny. These people, like, got their hair done,'" Carlos said.

Some of the comedians were determined not to be upstaged by the audience, so we had a local designer named Barbara Bates on tap to tailor-make suits for them to wear onstage. Barbara's office was next-door to All Jokes, and she designed clothes for many celebrities, including Oprah Winfrey, Michael Jordan, and Whitney Houston. The comedians she designed stage clothes for included Cedric the Entertainer, Steve Harvey, Bernie Mac, and Jonathan Slocumb.

Anyone who's been to an event with a predominantly black crowd knows it's not just the audience's fashion sense that's on point. African Americans have very discerning taste. Suffice it to say, we're not easily impressed.

Aries Spears said in *Phunny Business*, "Black people don't give a damn about effort: 'We paid to get in, you forced us to buy two drinks.' Dude just bought some hot wings. He found out 20 minutes into the show that this date he's with ain't gonna give him none, so he's mad. And now it's on you."

Our customers were tough critics, but the comedians could give as good as they got. If anyone was bold enough to sit near the stage, they best have had nerves of steel. We typically seated the front rows last because no one wanted to sit there, fearful that the comedians would put them on blast. Little did they know that the comedians hung out near the lobby and observed the audience closely before they went on, and it was then that they would select whom they wanted to tease. However, sitting in front did come with its own special risk. There was always the bold soul who thought that they were funny and would rush to the front. Suffice it to say, they'd often be massacred.

As George Carlin said, "I think it's the duty of the comedian to find out where the line is drawn and cross it deliberately."

Joe Torry was the best at insults. He had thousands of them. I recall one incident with a lady who sat up front and wouldn't stop talking loudly and disrupting the show. Joe proceeded to crush her.

God forbid a white person had the nerve to sit up front. I specifically instructed the comedians not to pick on the white folk. I thought it was a hack move, a cheap laugh, and it usually came directly at the customer's expense. But George Willborn was one of the few who was truly good at it. He'd ask a white lady, "Do you have any black in you? No? Do you want some?" It worked every time.

As the '90s wore on and word spread about All Jokes throughout the comedy industry, we began to attract performers of all races who wanted to try out their material in front of audiences who would give them honest feedback. White comedians would call me on a daily basis. People who feel they're good at something, especially art and music, want to prove themselves in front of an African American audience. That's why Mick Jagger studied James Brown. (Of course, Mick Jagger ain't never gon' be James Brown.)

One thing I've found to be true in business is that investing in quality pays dividends. The caliber of talent we had at All Jokes attracted the elite from the worlds of entertainment and sports to come through our doors. Many black celebrities frequented All Jokes. On a given night, you might see R. Kelly, Vivica A. Fox, or MC Lyte. Regular customers also included radio personalities like Tom Joyner and Doug Banks.

It also wasn't unusual to see sports stars in the audience such as Michael Jordan and his first wife, Juanita, as well as Scottie Pippen, Juwan Howard, Barry Sanders, Thomas Hearns, and a host of others. Many of the Bears of that era were regulars: Wilber Marshall, Otis Wilson, Willie Gault, Mike Singletary, Richard Dent, Chris Zorich.

We made sure our audience was well taken care of—after all, they paid their hard-earned money to be there. But I didn't believe in offering comp tickets to celebrities. For one, I soon realized that a celebrity appearance on a particular night didn't necessarily guarantee a bump in ticket sales the next. Chicago audiences were savvy enough to know that a star, like lightning, wasn't likely to strike in the same place twice. And, more importantly, the rich and famous had ample means to cover their tabs. Why should I offer them free admission and free drinks when they earned more than we made at the club? Don't get me wrong; I loved having celebrities come by the club—just not the ones who insisted on being comped. It was as simple as this: supporting black business meant no comps.

Everyone was welcome at All Jokes. We didn't have any velvet ropes separating the common folk from the VIPs. We created an inclusive environment, which I felt benefited the comedians as much as the fans. For many of our regular customers, All Jokes was a place to mark birthdays, anniversaries, and other special occasions. There were even times when men popped the question to their unsuspecting girlfriends, to the delight of everyone else in the audience. All Jokes became a celebratory place, a place that you had to visit when you came to Chicago.

James and I were in business to make money, but we didn't want to price ourselves out of the market. For most shows, admission was about $20, and drinks were about $10 in today's dollars. We wanted the All Jokes experience to be a relatively affordable one so that catching a show at our club could be a date night for a working-class cat and his lady or a ladies night for a group of girlfriends who simply wanted to hang out and laugh.

Thus, for a relatively small amount of money, customers could see up close many performers who later became big stars. But it was also a great place to go and hang out on a

Saturday night. We wanted comedy fans to frequent All Jokes not only to see laugh-out-loud standup but also to enjoy the atmosphere. I always felt it was a great place to take a date. The comedians took a little of the pressure off. It was a really upscale, cool vibe with a room full of well-dressed, beautiful people—a place where you could feel comfortable holding hands and acting romantic. I even had a few dates there myself.

On a typical night, the makeup of the audience was about 80 percent black, 15 percent Latino, and 5 percent white and "other." Sometimes people would just pop in because they were staying at a hotel in the Loop and they heard about the comedy club that was nearby. Our inclusive environment policy resulted in some interesting seating combinations. A minister who was a pillar of the community might be seated next to a street hustler. One thing about black folk is that we are all just one generation removed from one another. I don't care how successful you are, or how far you've come from the projects—all of us have a "Pookie" in our family.

A comedian could look out into the audience and see his doctor at one table, his drug dealer at the next, his girlfriend at the next, and his college professor at the table next to her. The comedians had to develop their act and material to be universal. As we showcased more comedians from different walks of life, the audience began to diversify even further as well. Everyone was there to have a good time, but that's not to say there weren't tense moments here and there. The protocol I always followed was that first and foremost, the show was on the stage, not in the audience. Steve Harvey used to say, "When you came in the door, they gave you a ticket and me the mic; that's a clue."

Wednesday was open-mic night, and we strove for the vibe of *Showtime at the Apollo.* It was my attempt at giving true amateurs a place to develop and grow, as well as veterans a time to work on their acts. But the audiences could be brutal. If the audience didn't like your act, they would shake their keys loudly until the host came to get you. The host had to be a strong comedian to manage that crowd and keep things from getting out of hand. Adele Givens, a true West Side of Chicago girl, held it down with grace. She would curse your ass out and embarrass you so badly that you might not come back next week. That went for performers as well. She was boss. After her career took off, she went on the road and Damon Williams—who can now be heard doing the "Seriously Ignorant News" on the *Tom Joyner Morning Show*—took over hosting open-mic nights. Damon, who is from the South Side, had a smoother approach, but it was very effective, and we did not miss a beat when he took over.

One night, things got a little bumpy when one outspoken customer decided to challenge our no-heckling policy. A group of young guys came in, and right from the start, we could see trouble coming. They were loud and disrespectful at the box office. While I was not worried, I did put our security guys on alert.

The rowdy young guys continued their act once they were seated, trying to outshine the performers by being "funny" and talking back to the stage. They kept screaming, "Thug life!" The staff gave the guys a couple of warnings, which they proceeded to ignore. One member of the group was especially vocal. He continued to heckle, so we finally said, "Sir, you got to go." He went off. We escorted him out. He made a move that looked he might be going for a weapon.

Fortunately, the off-duty cops that were around that night were attentive. Their presence always cut down on a lot of bullshit. On this occasion, when the heckler got out of control, one of the off-duty police officers stepped in to contain the situation.

He came up to me and said, "Do you want me to handle this?"

I said, "Please."

When the heckler appeared to reach for a weapon, the off-duty police officer promptly pulled out a 9 mm handgun. While I appreciated the protection, that made me all kinds of nervous. I was afraid the incident would spiral into a shootout. I saw my professional career flashing before me— "Man shot dead at All Jokes Aside." The guy, being young, said to the officer, "You think this the first time I had a gun in my face? Shoot me."

Time seemed to stop as I watched this shit go down, wondering if I was going to lose everything I'd worked so hard to build because of one heckler. Eventually, his boys said, "Man, come on, let's get out of here."

My guy came up to me later and said, "Ray, let me tell you something. If this wasn't All Jokes Aside, I would have shot him, point blank."

Another tense moment came when an irate customer threatened to disrupt Chris Rock's headlining engagement. The customer went crazy when he arrived to find that tickets had sold out. But the staff had told him when he called earlier in the day that he should get to the box office early since Chris's show would mostly likely sell out.

We didn't take reservations. I had learned that it's really hard to do reservations with black people because, in cultural terms, we don't really have a lot of respect for time. This phenomenon, I've observed, applies not only to social gatherings among family and friends but also to formal affairs, church services, weddings, funerals, and live entertainment events of all sorts. In my experience, black folk think that a reservation means they can come any time you want to. It doesn't. If someone didn't show up by halfway through the show, for whatever reason, they lost their money, and I had the right to sell the seat. The ticket was only part of the revenue stream—someone being late meant I lost drink sales as well. Folks just did not understand that. To avoid hassles, we sold tickets on a first come, first served basis.

We also maintained a ticketing system, even though it required doing a little more work than some of the other clubs. Carolines, for example, had the most efficient system in the business. One, it allowed reservations; two, there were no tickets, just slips of paper with numbers on them. Customers were led to a table, and at the end of the show, they'd get a bill for everything: the tickets, the food, and the drinks.

I could never do that at All Jokes. If a brother got his full bill all at once and saw that he had just spent $100, all of a sudden, that show was not that funny. So I had to break the costs up: customers would pay for the tickets at the box office and pay for the drinks at the table.

Philip Bailey of Earth, Wind & Fire fame made the same observation about black ticket buyers in his 2014 autobiography, *Shining Star*. As EW&F experienced increasing crossover success in the late '70s, Bailey wrote, "we began to notice our core audience shifting dramatically. We were drawing a lot more white fans because of the realities of disposable income. Whites, who could more easily afford the tickets, tended to order their seats in advance; traditionally, black audiences were more likely to 'walk up.'"

So while this customer who wanted to take his girlfriend to see Chris Rock had been informed that tickets were sold in person and that the box office was open from 9 a.m. until show time, he was apparently surprised when he showed up just before the show started to find that the event was indeed sold out.

I told him, "Our box office has been open since 9 this morning."

He was like, "You know what? Ain't gonna be no fuckin' show tonight!"

Police headquarters was just around the corner at 11th and State Streets, literally one block away from All Jokes. I happened to be in the lobby talking to two off-duty police officers attending Chris's show that night who were ready to step in. And man, was I glad they were there! This customer was going off. They looked at him, and they looked at me. I sort of shrugged at the officers like, *What should I do?* Before I knew it, they escorted him out the door. Next thing I knew, this dude was in handcuffs in the car going to jail.

Once again, I had narrowly escaped a nightmare scenario of my business becoming a crime scene. Looking back now, I see that incident as an example of how wildly successful All Jokes had become by the mid 1990s.

When I reflect on that story, I think, here's a guy who went to work in the morning, heard Chris Rock on the radio, called his lady, and said, "Let's go see Chris Rock tonight at All Jokes Aside." She was excited and started telling her friends at work and thinking about what she was going to wear, and he was thinking, "Oh, what a night this is going to be . . . ." Everyone was psyched—only he ended up spending the night in jail for disorderly conduct and threatening a police officer. The extremes folks would go to if they couldn't get into All Jokes Aside!

8

WHO'S LAUGHING NOW?

Do you have to say grace over leftovers? —DEON COLE

BY THE MID 1990s, after we'd been in business about three years, All Jokes Aside had become *the* place to see headlining standup comedians of color with national reputations in a first-class venue. Many of the headliners eventually got their big breaks in movies and TV as a result of the exposure they received at All Jokes. One sure sign that All Jokes had achieved this level of success came when competitors began to copy the business model James and I had so carefully crafted.

"There were other people in Chicago trying to do the same thing, trying to copy it," said All Jokes regular Kim Rudd, a Chicago advertising executive. "They'd do a comedy night at a club, and it didn't have the same feel; it was manufactured. It was kind of lowbrow, quite frankly. You know, you got guys onstage that were just cussing and doing the whole shock value thing."

"During that time, there were not many black[-owned] comedy clubs at all," comedian Tony Sculfield said in *Phunny Business*. "You could count them on one hand: you had All Jokes in Chicago and Detroit, the Comedy Act in LA and Atlanta, Steve Harvey's Comedy House in Dallas, and Uptown Comedy Club also in Atlanta, and that's it. There were probably about five in the entire nation that were serving African American comedy audiences, and All Jokes Aside owned two of them. It felt good to have that here in the city of Chicago because with only five in the country, you know African American comics had five cities in which to perform. So to have one right here in my own backyard was absolutely fantastic and instrumental to my career."

When I was first starting out, I thought that with such small numbers involved, it stood to reason that we black-owned entertainment businesses could band together to maximize our limited resources and offer each other mutual support, as people do in Jewish, Asian, and other minority communities. Why not book talent as a group and negotiate better deals for us all? Why compete with each other in the same markets when there were potentially 25 markets around the country that were primed for a club? Why not divide it up and conquer? But too often in the African American community, such solidarity is not the norm.

Don't take it from me; just pick up a television remote control and do a little channel surfing to see competition through imitation. Black Entertainment Television made broadcasting history when it launched on January 25, 1980, as the first cable channel with programming geared specifically toward African American audiences. But clicking through the channels nowadays, you'll see competitors such as TV One, Centric, and Bounce. NBA legend Earvin "Magic" Johnson has even ventured into the cable television arena with the ASPiRE network, as has Oprah Winfrey with OWN (although, the Oprah Winfrey Network is marketed as a lifestyle channel aimed primarily at women of all races, not just African Americans).

So when word of All Jokes's success spread across the industry, my competitors were not about to sit back and let me have all that comedy gold to myself. In Chicago, Steve Harvey had put us on the map with more than just the customers. His radio prowess put us front and center for all types of people. We'd get an odd visitor inquiring about our business and what we were up to, but the same guy never came by twice. Looking back on it, I'm not sure if they were underworld figures—it kinda felt that way, but I think we got lucky in that regard.

However, nearby nightclub the Clique was run by soul brothers with Deep South ties, and they offered anything but friendly competition. We had been open about six months and were starting to build momentum when I got a visit from one of the Clique's owners, who tried to "convince" me to cut a profit-sharing deal. He came by several times and made several pitches, but I had no interest. I had a partner, and I had not quit my job and bet it all to realize someone else's vision. The co-owner of the Clique was not too happy with my decision, and he finally came to me with a message that either I partner with them or I'd be out of business.

The Clique was located about a mile south of All Jokes Aside. It was one of the hottest clubs in the city. Situated on two floors, it was a massive space. It was a very popular spot featuring the best deejays and live bands. It was the go-to club for professional athletes, entertainers, and local celebrities. To my knowledge, they never did comedy. But shortly after we opened, they would do a "Comedy Clique" show on Friday and Saturday nights, featuring local acts.

Shortly after I refused to cut the Clique folks a profit-sharing deal, and I'm not saying that they had anything to do with it, we began to get a visit virtually every night from some city authority—usually either the police department or the fire department. If one of the bulbs was out in my exit lights, we got a fine. Fortunately, we created a nice following fairly quickly. As I said, there were policemen coming to the club and enjoying themselves, and we had a few regular firemen as well. By this time, we had paid our respects and shared our long-term plan with the alderman, who became a staunch supporter, and there were other city officials who came to the club and who enjoyed and respected what we were doing.

The Clique figured that they had a better space. At the time, they did—they had a nightclub with all of the bells and whistles, and though the operations were just okay, they did have a liquor license. I'm sure they thought that the only thing I had that they didn't was the talent. And given their connections to the entertainment world, they could get that. So they proceeded to attack us with that competitive advantage. They tried to book the comedians who were drawing crowds at All Jokes. They'd even come to shows at our club and go directly to the comedians, invite them to the Clique, then put them in the VIP section and introduce them to fine women and who knows what else. It was a good idea, but I had built exclusivity clauses into our agreements with many comics. If I was going to invest in building a comedian's brand in the Chicago marketplace and develop a following for him, then I felt that we were partners. Some of the comics didn't like that. One called me an "imperialist of comedy." Some said I was denying them the ability to work. I told them this: "I'm not denying you anything. You can work wherever you like, but Michael Jordan can't play for the Chicago Bulls one week and then next week play for the Detroit Pistons. You have to choose. If you choose to be with me, I'm exclusive. It's you and me against the world."

Once again, I relied on the relationships I was building when I asked the comedians to remain loyal to the All Jokes brand. The way I saw it, not only would exclusivity honor the relationships I'd established with the comedians but it also just made good business sense. By asking for loyalty from the performers, I was only doing what a wise business-man like Motown mogul Berry Gordy would do. If a slew of record companies had sprung up in Detroit when Motown became an international success in the '60s, would Gordy have agreed to let Diana Ross and The Supremes, Stevie Wonder, Marvin Gaye, and other top acts release records on competing labels and then come back to Motown whenever they pleased?

While most of the comedians saw the logic in the exclu-sivity clause, one who didn't was Sheryl Underwood. Born in Little Rock, Arkansas, Sheryl grew up in Chicago and went on to fame as one of the panelists on the CBS show *The Talk*, and as one of the few black Republicans in the entertainment industry—or anywhere, for that matter! Sheryl honed her standup skills in Chicago with many appearances at All Jokes Aside.

"I can tell you Chicago was really the . . . laboratory in which my style of comedy was evolving," Sheryl told the *Chicago Tribune* in a 1993 profile. "No female that I knew of at the time was doing what I was doing."

The *Chicago Tribune* story promoted Sheryl's appearance at one of our competitors, a comedy club called Jokers Wild that opened only a couple blocks south of All Jokes.

"My motivation was for it to be an alternative to All Jokes Aside," Jokers Wild owner Reggie Norman told the *Chicago Tribune*. "I really felt Chicago could really stand another black comedy club."

Interestingly, Jokers Wild was located on the second floor of Club United Nations at 17 East Balbo Avenue in a renovated space that for a few weeks in the summer of 1993 was the home of another of our competitors: the Comedy Act Theater.

The fact that Comedy Act Theater founder Michael Williams had decided to try to compete with All Jokes was especially challenging. The Comedy Act Theater's Los Angeles club was where James and I had first been exposed to the wealth of black comedy talent. He was an inspiration. But James and I had always felt that we could create something better—and besides, there was enough for everybody. We had opened in Chicago, not LA. But according to Michael, Chicago was special. Chicago was the birthplace of the great Robin Harris, and Michael and Robin had always dreamed of returning to Robin's hometown and opening a club. Robin had died a year earlier, but Michael decided to open a Chicago club anyway. And he opened strong with Jamie Foxx as his first headliner.

But Michael was not on the best terms with many of the comedians who once appeared in his club. The positive relationships I'd developed with the comedians and their managers and agents proved to be a key factor. And I always felt that the Comedy Act Theater lacked the level of service and the attention to detail—benefiting both the comedians and the audience—that I was committed to achieving at All Jokes. Once again, this goes back to the importance of nurturing and maintaining relationships because when the comedians and the audiences had to choose, they chose All Jokes.

Furthermore, this was Chicago, my backyard. While I had a great deal of admiration and respect for what Michael had done in the past, I wasn't finna let him come into my house, snatch the food off of my table, and eat it right in front of me. I think that Michael underestimated not only us but the market as well. Chicago was a tough comedy market in which to compete. The mainstream clubs—The Improv and Zanies, in particular—competed aggressively for top talent, and the Comedy Clique survived by featuring local acts and headliners that I didn't book. Where was Michael going to fit in? What would be his unique selling proposition? He lasted maybe three or four months.

As I stated earlier, it wasn't just African American club owners who tried to siphon off our business. Once All Jokes took off, the mainstream clubs woke up to the fact that there was, indeed, a very strong demand for African American comedy. Zanies, The Improv, and the other big names weren't going to sit back and let me dominate this market unchallenged. When Chris Rock came to town, they wanted Chris Rock. When Dave Chappelle came to town, they wanted Dave Chappelle. When George Wallace came to town. . . . End result: the competition drove up the comedians' asking prices. On the surface, this was good for the comedians in the short term, but if all the clubs closed due to oversaturation and exorbitant prices, nobody won. As far as the audience went, this kind of result just meant higher ticket prices. Higher ticket prices typically result in lower bar revenue. Lower bar revenue leads to closure. A comedy club survives on bar revenue.

On occasion, I found myself in a bidding war over how much All Jokes and our mainstream counterparts could pay headliners. Oftentimes, if I was paying the same or more, we won out. I guess the comedians figured that if it was really close or a tie, they would go with me. If I could not compete, they'd go to the other club, as they should have.

Comedy tours—the Def Comedy Jam tour, in particular—were a direct competitor of ours, but at the same time, we fed off each other too. All Jokes may have been a bit slow the night a big show was in town, but for the most part, it all worked out. Such tours typically had four or five comedians doing 20 to 25 minutes per set. I would book each one of those same comedians for the next few months as headliners, giving them an opportunity to do their entire act of 45 minutes to an hour. The concert tour served as an infomercial of sorts for each comedian. That worked well—until everyone and their momma became a comedy tour promoter. After all, it only takes a little cash and a pen.

Producing a standup comedy show looks easy from the outside. It's not. These fly-by-night promoters drove prices to unsustainable levels, making it hard to book the top talent at a reasonable fee. Then, to add insult to injury, year after year, they'd be gone and the comics that spurned me were back at All Jokes's doorstep.

Then came TV. While not a direct competitor, it proved a challenge. Like the tours, the TV competition was a good thing—at first.

HBO's *Def Comedy Jam*, hosted by Martin Lawrence, was the king. My relationship with the show began in late 1991, when producer Bob Sumner approached me to put on a showcase at All Jokes Aside featuring the best standup comedians in Chicago. He predicted that *Def Comedy Jam* would be the hottest thing on TV when it premiered in early 1992. At the time, there were no shows featuring comedians of color. The idea was to pair standup comedy and hip-hop. HBO bought the show, and that was the perfect place for it because as a cable channel, it wasn't bound by the content and language restrictions of the broadcast networks. On HBO, comics could let loose with all of the foul language and blue material that they wanted. And they did.

Def Comedy Jam was a smash right from the start. In order to appear on the show, the comedians had to have a great seven minutes of material. It gave opportunity-poor comedians an outlet to showcase their talent to a national audience. And that audience wasn't just people of color. I once heard that 65 percent of *Def Jam*'s audience was white. It stood to reason, I thought, as that kind of strong white audience representation was also the case for blues, jazz, and most definitely hip-hop.

Partnering with *Def Jam* was great for All Jokes Aside. Every year, we held several showcases, and I would consult with Bob and offer my recommendations on comics I saw at All Jokes Aside who would fit well on *Def Jam*. I received a credit for as long as the show aired.

But not everybody dug it. Segments of the black community were appalled at the rawness of *Def Comedy Jam*. Bill Cosby was, unsurprisingly, among those who were not amused. *The Cosby Show* had brought a middle-class black family, with middle-class values, to national television, and it was the No. 1 show for four seasons. Its unprecedented crossover success proved that black comedians didn't have to rely on the racist caricatures of the past—caricatures that Cosby saw embodied in the humor of *Def Comedy Jam*. He spoke out publicly against host Martin Lawrence and the show itself, calling it a "minstrel show."

Others, too, were upset. In an op-ed piece in the *New York Daily News*, Stanley Crouch wrote, "Russell Simmons' *Def Comedy Jam* is the ultimate coon show update of human cesspools, where 'cutting edge' has come to mean traveling ever more downward in the sewer."

When Cosby and others tuned into *Def Comedy Jam*, they saw black performers playing the fool for white audiences, a relationship that Cosby and his generation of comedians had spent their lifetimes trying to destroy. The younger comics who appeared on the show wholly rejected these accusations. They were nobody's fools, and, as they saw it, they weren't hurting anybody.

In an interview, Lawrence took personal offense to Cosby's words: "Cosby needs to do a reality check and remember where he comes from. . . . He might not [use foul language], but somewhere in his roots, he has people in his family who did. Cosby can't throw that to me. Cuss words to me are just words. Where I come from, they're just words."

Later, *Def Comedy Jam*'s executive producer Russell Simmons remembered, "You know, the show got criticized and accused of a lot of shit by journalists and some blacks, who claimed it promoted negative images of black people. . . . The truth is, the comedians used their own real language. That's how they talk. Those were their jokes. It was their opportunity to do their routines, tell their jokes, and use their language just as they did in a club, except now they were on camera."

Like hip-hop artists, the comics were being real to the life that they and their audiences knew. Though not all of the comics who appeared on *Def Comedy Jam* had a strong hip-hop sensibility, there was no question that was a big part of the show and its appeal. The audience was always filled with members dressed in the current fashions—the most distinctive outfits in the crowd were consistently good material for the comedians onstage.

The comedians also made interesting fashion choices, including Chicago's own Bernie Mac. In addition to wearing a graffitied denim ensemble in a 1992 appearance, Mac wove the show's sensibility into his act. In a takeoff from the old-school comic bit of using the drummer to punctuate a punchline, Mac had the deejay drop a beat in place of a cymbal crash. Whether or not it was Simmons's intention,

Def Comedy Jam did change, for a time at least, audiences' expectations of black comics and, in turn, black comics' expectations of what audiences wanted to hear.

I never succumbed to the temptation to copy *Def Jam*'s success. I maintained our mission, which was to feature a variety of styles that matched the variety of our audiences. I also wove some of the acts together so that I always maintained a balance. If I had one of the cruder comedians like T.K. Kirkland headlining, I might have the cleaner Jonathan Slocumb as the host.

It required work to ensure that All Jokes did not morph into "Def Jam Live." You only had to have a strong seven-minute set to appear on *Def Comedy Jam*. You needed at least 45 minutes to headline a club. I insisted that comedians have more to say than, "That bitch better have my money," or "Give it up for all the pretty ladies in the house." All Jokes Aside gave the comedians an opportunity to avoid being pigeonholed into the raw, blue style. Better still, I thought, it was a place for people to go if they weren't into hip-hop. As it always had in the past, I knew that the trend of profanity-, sex-, and insult-based humor would eventually burn itself out. Ain't that many Joe Torrys, T.K. Kirklands, and D.L. Hughleys out there. Great blue humor takes intelligence, insight, and meaning; a string of curse words doesn't make for a very good joke.

That said, *Def Comedy Jam* was a very good thing for All Jokes. And I'd assert without hesitation that *Def Comedy Jam* was a very good thing for comedy overall. I am proud to have worked with Russell, Bob, director Stan Lathan (yet another distinguished member of Kappa Alpha Psi, I must note), and their entire team. There was no questioning the impact that *Def Comedy Jam* had on all parties involved. "As seen on *Def Comedy Jam*" became a must-have stamp of approval for most black comedians of that era. A stamp that the audiences came to expect.

BET's *Comic View* began as an alternative to *Def Comedy Jam*. *Comic View* aired from September 1992 to December 2008. The first season was taped live from comedy clubs, and All Jokes Aside was one of the first to be featured. It was great to have as many outlets as possible to showcase talent, but because they couldn't be as raw on *Comic View* since BET aired on basic cable, comedians had to adapt. Unlike *Def Comedy Jam*, *Comic View* didn't pay to fly comics out to LA for tapings of the show, nor did they pay a per diem. If a comedian was selected, he had to get himself to the show.

I never liked that. Why not compensate the talent? After all, BET was a billion-dollar company. This made it hard for a lot of talented comedians who simply did not have the means to make it to LA to appear on *Comic View*. I even wrote founder Bob Johnson, a fellow Kappa, about it. (No word yet.)

We would often sponsor a few cats with whom we had especially good relationships, covering their travel expenses to appear on *Comic View* as a gesture of support for their work. A funny story resulted when young comic Robert Hines was selected. This would not only be his first time on TV; it would also be his first time out of the state of Illinois. But Robert had no money to get to LA, so he came to me to

see if I could help in any way. I liked him a lot. He had started out as a doorman at All Jokes and worked himself up to a
solid 20 minutes of good material. He killed in his audition
and was ready to go. I told him that I would buy his airline
ticket and pay for one night in a motel. Steve Harvey slept
in his car when he was starting out, so as I saw it, a night in
a motel would be like the Ritz-Carlton for a new comic—
especially if it were free!

I gave Robert the number of our travel agent and told
him to call her, as she was taking care of the arrangements.

He looked at me quizzically and said, "What's a travel
agent?"

He had never heard of a travel agent, let alone been on a
plane. He was 30 years old. Truth be told, I had never heard
of a travel agent myself until I purchased my first plane ticket to attend Morehouse.

Comic View never reached the critical acclaim of *Def
Comedy Jam*, but it did well and was on the air for a longer
run than *Def Comedy Jam*. I worked directly with the producers of the show throughout the run of All Jokes Aside.

Around that time, I met Mark Adkins and his partner,
Andre Wiseman, at a Comic Relief benefit that we held at All
Jokes. Mark's brother, Sinbad, was the headliner that night.
Mark served as Sinbad's manager, and I booked a few comics
to open for him. The show was a hit.

That weekend, Mark and Andre came to a few shows
and were impressed with what we were doing. What I think
most impressed Mark was the variety of cats that we booked.
I ended up booking several of Mark's clients, including A.J.
Jamal and Geoff Brown.

Mark and I talked occasionally about a variety of sub-jects, including the possibility of him and Sinbad investing in our vision of a chain of black comedy clubs. That never materialized, but what did come out of it was the idea to pro-duce a true alternative to *Def Comedy Jam*: a conscious show for both comedians and audiences who wanted to do and see something different from what *Def Comedy Jam* and *Comic View* were doing. This format was a regular part of what we did at All Jokes, so I thought I knew what would work. It was simply a matter of taking what we did and transferring it to television.

I knew very little about TV other than what I had experi-enced working with *Def Comedy Jam* and *Comic View*. I did have an interest in producing, and I felt very confident that I could produce a show on par with, if not better than, both *Def Comedy Jam* and *Comic View*. And I could keep it clean.

Mark and his contacts at Comedy Central were intrigued by the concept. Laurie Zaks, head of the network's original programming department, agreed to fly in to Chicago and see what we were talking about. I was charged with setting up a showcase for Laurie. I lined up my best acts that were very funny but could work clean. Laurie was blown away, and she bought the show on the spot. The new show, called *Comic Justice*, went on the air in summer 1993.

"'Comic Justice' Makes Jokes, Not War, On Life," read the headline of an August 1993 story penned by Allan John-son of the *Chicago Tribune*. "'Comic Justice' probably will be called a clean version of 'Def Jam,' a show known for its raunchy language and themes," the story read. "But 'Comic Justice' takes a more positive approach, according to its producers, talent and Comedy Central executives."

The article quoted *Comic Justice* host A.J. Jamal saying, "I think the importance of this show is to educate and inform our viewing audience to the fact that blacks are not just a 'Def Jam' type of group. We don't just curse and tap dance."

The *Tribune* article concluded, "'Comic Justice' was taped last spring at Chicago's All Jokes Aside. It showcases standup comics whose material is virtually free of profanity."

We taped 13 episodes at All Jokes, and the show was a legitimate hit on Comedy Central. It was a refreshing alternative to *Def Comedy Jam*. In addition to Jamal, *Comic Justice* featured Dave Chappelle, J. Anthony Brown, Michael Colyar, and, of course, Sinbad. A host of the All Jokes posse also appeared, including George Willborn, Tony Sculfield, Deon Cole, Godfrey, and James Hannah. These talented comedians made the show a hit.

And yet, the show almost didn't happen. In my opinion, All Jokes Aside and the city of Chicago were critical assets to the show. I had expected to be actively involved and receive an executive producer credit. But the effort to develop the show became so contentious that I was ready to pull the plug and walk away a few days before the first taping was scheduled to take place. I ultimately reached an agreement with Laurie Zaks and the Comedy Central folks in the final hours. While I'm not cool with how it all went down, in the end I'm proud of the shows that took place at All Jokes Aside—shows to which we made a significant contribution. I'm proud of the opportunity that the comedians received.

I managed to maintain a great relationship with Laurie, and—as silly as it may sound—we got an amazing backdrop design out of it, created by the legendary production designer Naomi Slodki.

Despite the success of *Comic Justice*, the producers, to my disappointment, decided to move the show to LA for its second season. In my opinion, it just wasn't the same. It lacked the energy that we had at All Jokes Aside. And as it turned out, the show was canceled after the second season.

I was disenchanted by the whole *Comic Justice* experience, but I still felt that *Comic View* left a lot to be desired. So I figured, *I know this game as well, if not better, than anyone. So why not do my own show?* I planned to tape the show at All Jokes and syndicate it around the country.

No one had done a weekly syndicated standup show before. I had a roster of cats who I thought could pull it off: Pierre, T.K. Kirkland, Rodney Winfield, and, locally, Deon Cole, Damon Williams, B. Cole, and Corey Holcomb. When called upon, they were talented enough to work clean. It would be like when The Temptations sang Sinatra. While they made their living singing R&B, they were talented enough to sing Sinatra and do it (in my father's opinion at least) *better* than Sinatra.

I booked George Wallace to host the *All Jokes Aside* TV show. To direct, I hired Darryl Roberts, a Chicago-based producer and director with a few good credits under his belt. I went all out, bringing on a cinematographer whose day job was *The Oprah Winfrey Show* and a top editor from Trio Video. For the first show, we taped two evenings at All Jokes. Both were sold out and the shows were amazing.

It cost about $75,000 in today's dollars to produce the *All Jokes Aside* TV show, but I was certain that we had a hit. We purchased an hour on the local NBC affiliate, and we did well. The show's ratings were strong in both the black and general markets. We even had an overture from the local ABC affiliate for a weekly *All Jokes Aside* series. But we didn't sell enough ads to cover our production costs. I lost my ass on that one. I had been naïve. Producing for TV was harder than it looked.

9

DETOUR THROUGH THE MOTOR CITY

I don't mean to sound bitter, cold, or cruel, but I am, so that's the way it comes out.

—BILL HICKS

THE FACT THAT CHICAGO EMBRACED All Jokes Aside was gratifying, but I had a grander vision for the business. Even before we opened the club, I dreamed of All Jokes Aside becoming a national chain like The Improv. My ultimate goal would have been to be in a dozen cities. I envisioned an entertainment company with $30 million in annual revenues.

Moreover, building an All Jokes Aside chain would prove that we didn't just have a home court advantage with the original Chicago location, and that its runaway success wasn't beginner's luck. As All Jokes flourished, I delved deeper into my efforts to create a chain. Expanding would prove our Chicago success was no fluke. You're not a real entrepreneur, they say, until you've done it at least twice.

My first choice for where to expand with a second location was Washington, DC. James was from the area (his family still lived there), and there were strong Morehouse and Kappa presences in DC. The DC metro area had an affluent black middle class and a great group of local comedians, including Tony Woods, Teddy Carpenter, Chris Thomas, Red Grant, and Joe Clair.

In 1993, we found a great space in a class "A" general office building in downtown DC, signed a letter of intent and hired an architect. I rented an apartment in DC. Mary pounded the pavement during the day to get the club up and running, and I commuted from Chicago a few days every week to oversee the overall progress.

We were knee-deep into the project when we began to get concerned that the lease negotiations were taking way too long. We were almost done with the architectural drawings and we had begun our marketing and promotional plan. We had started speaking with local groups in DC about hosting special events at the new club. But we still hadn't signed a lease.

Eventually, we got a call from the landlord to schedule a meeting. We figured this was finally it, and we summoned our lawyer, Stuart Savitz, from Chicago. We were prepared to sign the final lease agreement. But the landlord wanted to meet for a different reason. He said he wanted to see our plans before signing off—but we had already provided the plans, which had been approved. At the 11th hour, the landlord had received concerns from other tenants that a comedy club was not the right fit for the building.

"Why is that?" I asked. "We've been at this for over six months. What's up? It's an office building, where most all tenants leave by the time we get started." After all, we had started out working after hours in an office building in Chicago and had operated there without incident. We threatened to sue, but the landlord decided to return all of the capital investment that we had made to date.

We were so disenchanted with the whole ordeal that I began to look at what was supposed to be the third location in my master plan: Detroit. I was going solo on this one. James and Mary had no interest in the Detroit market, but I was convinced that it was a sleeping giant. It helped that the city was less than an hour plane ride from Chicago, among other advantages.

Detroit has birthed some of the best names in comedy. A very short list of Motor City comedy notables includes Gilda Radner, Lily Tomlin, Johnny Carson's *Tonight Show* sidekick Ed McMahon, David Alan Grier, and *Home Improvement* star Tim Allen. Detroit's black comedy scene was very strong, with the legendary Downtown Tony Brown, Mike Bonner, Tony Roberts, COCO, Cool Aide, Karen Addison, and a host of others who I felt made the city almost as strong as Chicago.

With this kind of foundation to build on, Detroit seemed like the perfect spot. I conducted market research that confirmed opening in Detroit made perfect sense. After all, Detroit was a predominantly African American city with plenty of patrons with disposable income who would pay good money to see nationally known headliners. My research uncovered a 1990 study identifying trends in the comedy industry. The study seemed to confirm that Detroit was, indeed, a booming market for the standup scene.

"An attractive venue in a lighted and secured location, provided it is creatively programmed and professionally operated, would almost certainly flourish in downtown Detroit," the study concluded.

I called my Morehouse fraternity brother, Brian McGluan, who was a residential real estate broker in Detroit. Brian introduced me to Terry Edmondson, a commercial agent, and Terry took me around the entire city of Detroit searching for the right location. After about a month of searching, I found the right location in the theater district at 2036 Woodward Avenue, directly across the street from the world-famous Fox Theatre.

Owned by Chuck Forbes, a very successful and well-known real estate developer with a love for the arts, it was a great space. It had been a nightclub called 2036 and already had a liquor license. It was a stand-alone, three-story building with a separate space for a reception area, a stage level, and a lower-level space that made for a great green room and lounge for the comedians. Moreover, it was a familiar address for potential customers. The nightclub had ultimately failed, but for a brief period, it had been very popular with black folk. With the major build-out essentially done (unlike the complete rehab that we had needed in Chicago), it was a simple matter of retrofitting the space for our use.

After a month-long negotiation, Mr. Forbes and I entered into an agreement to bring All Jokes Aside to Detroit.

"This is a city that has a huge Black population, and I didn't see any comedy clubs in the area, that had been set up specifically for this market, so I brought All Jokes Aside in," Mr. Forbes said in the *Detroit Free Press* in June 1995. "It brings a diverse population to the center of our city. It's just good business."

Mr. Forbes became a trusted adviser and reminded me very much of my godfather, Mr. Crawford. I think that I reminded him of his younger self, a young gun trying to be a player. Initially, we got along great.

I enlisted Ben Ross, one of the managers at All Jokes Chicago, to relocate to Detroit and help me get the new venture up and running. Fortunately, Ben was game. He had a ton of experience with opening new clubs. He was excited about venturing to a new city, and he'd never been to Detroit before.

But right away, signs cropped up that opening a comedy club in the heart of Detroit might not be as easy as I thought. Finding qualified staff that could rise to the standards we'd established in Chicago was like trying to cast the lead in a blockbuster from a group of extras. We interviewed hundreds of people, but I soon learned Detroit has a different vibe when it comes to time. If the plumber told you he'd be there at 3 p.m., it could be 3 p.m. next week. Ben called it "Tomorrow Land."

It wasn't as though Ben wasn't used to a Midwestern pace. He grew up in Olathe, Kansas, and his first comedy club job was at Bushwackers Comedy Invasion in Manhattan, Kansas. He had also worked at both The Improv and The Funny Firm in Chicago. But people seemed to move much more slowly in Detroit than in Chicago. Detroiters that I encountered had a slow-moving, almost southern sensibility. And I had thought Chicago was slow after living in New York and working on Wall Street! Even stocking the Detroit club with alcohol was different from how it was in

Chicago. We had to buy the liquor from the state of Michigan, which added another frustrating layer of bureaucracy to our operations.

But I loved Detroit. Still do. I've always felt that despite its shortcomings, it has the potential to once again be a first-class American city. At the time we opened in late 1994, metro Detroit had the fourth-largest African American population in America. There were more than 750,000 African Americans in Detroit alone.

And politically, black folks ran the city. I had read a lot about Coleman Young and several of my uncles had worked in the auto plants in Detroit. I also knew the city had an enviable entertainment history, as well as one of the country's most profitable concert markets, and all of the arts were well represented. After all, it was the birthplace of Motown. Opening a comedy club there should have been a no-brainer.

After much work and planning, All Jokes Detroit officially opened in November 1994. Because the Detroit venture was so new and I had a tight deadline to get the club open, we didn't have time to install some of the state-of-the-art equipment, such as point-of-sale machines, that helped us keep track of ticket sales, alcohol, food, and other inventory at the Chicago club. But in spite of the challenges, we had fun setting up shop in Detroit. It was like we were pioneers exploring new territory.

Shortly before we opened in Detroit, James introduced me to Stacey Gray, who agreed to help out part time with the club's administrative business. She was a godsend. Meticulous, detail-oriented, and very organized, she was the best. Her "part-time" job at All Jokes was at least 40 hours a week, and she had a full-time job managing a $1 billion mutual fund. She was my Michael Jordan.

When I tell people now how hard Stacey worked, they don't believe me. She got to the bank at 7 a.m. because the money markets opened at 8 a.m. She left at 5 p.m. and headed to All Jokes to meet the bar-back at 5:30 p.m. (The bar-back's job is to set up the bar for the bartenders, ensuring that the bar is properly stocked, the beer is cold, the glasses are clean, and each lime wedge fits neatly inside a Corona bottle.) On Wednesdays and Thursdays, she was there until about 9:30 p.m. On Fridays and Saturdays, she'd be there until we closed at about 1:30 a.m., and on Sundays until 9:30 p.m.

When she got home on Sunday night, it would take her a couple of hours to prepare the deposits for Monday morning. Monday morning, she made the deposits, ordered liquor for the week, and prepared my weekend reports. She often joked that I'd call her on Monday morning for a report while she was trying to invest $100 million. "I'm sorry to bother you, but may I have the report on ticket sales by day and show, drink sales by day and show, and any customer or staffing issues I need to be aware of?" *What a dick.* I just couldn't wait for her to call me.

If not for Stacey, it would have been a much, much more difficult transition for Ben and me. She became my confidante. To this day, I don't make any important decisions without consulting with her first.

If Stacey was Michael Jordan, Ben was Scottie Pippen. And he was definitely discovering a whole new world. The comedians were already familiar with him from Chicago, and the staff and customers adored him instantly. Ben was a true bar aficionado, and he and a few of the other staff would go out practically every night after we closed. How they did it, I have no idea. I suppose if you don't have to work until noon, you can do that type of shit. He soon found out, however, that although the Detroit nightclubs and bars tend to close earlier than Chicago's, an alternate universe springs to life after hours—a universe in which he picked up the affectionate nickname "White Boy Ben."

I found out just how popular Ben had become in this world when he insisted that I go out to have a drink after work one night—at 1:30 a.m. I was hesitant; I didn't typically fraternize with the staff because it's not a good practice. *But what the fuck? We had a great night. It's Saturday—or should I say Sunday?—whatever, I don't have to be at the club until Sunday evening. Besides, I've got my second wind, I'm wide-awake, and—who knows?—might be a few cuties at this joint.*

As soon as we arrived—in fact, on the way there—I immediately noticed some shady characters and some questionable activities going down, and that's putting it mildly. I'm from East 28th Street; I know what it looks like when some shit could jump off at any minute.

I'm looking at Ben like, *Where the fuck are you taking me? You do know this is the 'hood, right?*

Ben says in his Kansas accent, "It's all good; they are cool people."

Folks ran up to hug and greet Ben like he was Prince Charles. *Really?* I didn't drink, dance, or talk to anybody. I was thinking, *This place is fucked up. One way in and one way out. How come the police and fire inspectors don't visit this spot? Oh, they are here . . . in the back drinking and gambling.* I stood by the door, head on a swivel all night. You would have thought that *I* was the white boy! The brothers we encountered were hardcore, gangsters for sure. And as for the cuties, I could swear that each one of them had a visible bullet-wound scar.

One of the more "attractive" ones came up to me and said, "I've never seen you here before. Can I get you anything?"

I smiled and said, "No, thank you," but I was thinking, *You can help me get the fuck outta here!*

But I was cool. I had to be because I couldn't leave right away—that would have been seen as disrespectful. It would have been ironic, however, if after all that I'd been through to avoid this type of shit at All Jokes, I was killed at 4 in the morning at Sugar Daddy's after-hours spot.

When we left, I told Ben, "Dude, you had to be drunk taking me to that spot. Are you crazy?"

"I must have been," Ben confessed, "to bring you to that place."

I love Ben, but I never hung out with him again.

Despite these side trips to the after-hours joints, I knew Ben was someone I could trust to keep the business running smoothly in Detroit when I was in Chicago. As for the on-stage talent, I recruited Detroit native Mike Bonner to be the emcee of All Jokes Detroit. Mike was a regular at the Chicago club, and he was a very funny, responsible, and coachable cat that I could depend on to fill this important role. He was not as in-your-face as George Willborn, but he was just as effective in handling the hosting duties. As the club's permanent host, he took advantage of the opportunity to network with and learn from his show-business peers.

"I enjoyed seeing the other comedians—the A.J. Jamals, the Steve Harveys—and knowing where I was in comparison to their acts," Mike told me. "I knew where I stood. I stood with the best. I still look for that energy I had during the All Jokes Aside days. That was a major time in urban comedy in America."

Just as in Chicago, I hired top headliners like Chris Rock, Steve Harvey, Cedric The Entertainer, D.L. Hughley, JB Smoove, Craig Robinson, Deon Cole, and Mo'Nique to fill the bill at All Jokes Detroit. My vision was for the club to provide top-of-the-line entertainment and service like Detroit had never seen.

Before our opening weekend, we decided not to have any kind of soft opening.

"There was no Wednesday show, no Thursday night show to try out different things," Ben said. "We'd do three shows Saturday night. It's bam, bam, bam! Get 'em in and out. In Chicago, we kind of built up to that over a year or so."

In retrospect, taking a more gradual approach may have been a better strategy to test out the new market. But I could not afford it. I was undercapitalized from the start. I needed to hit the ground running. Moreover, it may not have been the wisest choice to roll out the new club during the holiday season, which tends to be a slower time of year for the comedy business because potential customers are preoccupied with shopping, holiday parties, family get-togethers, and other seasonal activities.

By January 1995, after being open in Detroit for just two months, the stress of running two clubs in two different cities was already beginning to get to me. An entry from my journal dated New Year's Day 1995 summed up how I was feeling at the time: "The last weeks of December 1994 proved to be the most challenging of my career. It was a time of lows and mo' lows. At times, I feel I will come out of this with flying colors, then I recognize all of the strategic mistakes I made in this deal."

For the first time in the history of All Jokes Aside, I had to cancel a special show due to low ticket sales. I simply did not have the budget to market and promote the show, and as the new kid on the block, I got lost in the sauce. It didn't help that the Fox Theatre, a 5,000-seat-venue, had a huge show that night featuring many of the comics that I had once featured, including Bernie Mac. The canceled engagement at All Jokes Detroit resulted in a "disappointed comedian, disappointed staff, and a few bounced checks," I wrote in my journal. "It is not the way to enter a market, but perhaps it will work out to be a learning experience."

Just as when we opened All Jokes in Chicago, I invested my own money in the Detroit venture. This time, however, I was on my own; James and Mary were plotting their own solo ventures. I obtained a small bank loan instead of finding outside investors—a move that, right away, seemed questionable.

"As I reflect," I wrote in my journal that New Year's Day, "I remember a producer telling me, 'O.P.M.: Other People's Money. Once you've proven yourself, you never risk your own capital.'"

To make matters worse, Ben and other staff who initially had been gung ho about the adventure of opening in a new city began to question if the club was in the right location. Another entry in my journal from that time describes this winter of our discontent, so to speak: "There is a lot of second guessing on our expansion plans. It is my baby, and I feel a lot of people would be happy to see me fail. The troops are down and beginning to question the potential. I have even asked myself if I did the right thing."

A major pothole I hadn't foreseen while making our way to Detroit was competition from an existing comedy club—if it could be called that.

Bea's Comedy Kitchen, located at 541 East Larned Street in downtown Detroit, was a white-owned establishment that started out as a restaurant that catered to the mainstream crowd. But after experiencing a downturn in profits as an increasing number of white Detroiters fled to the suburbs, Bea's reinvented itself as a comedy club targeting minority consumers.

"Because of the boom in black comedy," Mike Bonner said, "it became a predominantly black club."

Bea's proved to be surprisingly stiff competition for All Jokes Detroit. Though I'd invested the same meticulous care in making the Detroit club an upscale, first-rate establishment, like the Chicago flagship, the decidedly low-rent Bea's continued to thrive.

To put it bluntly, Bea's was a dump. This isn't just me hating. And it had nothing to do with the fact that Bea was white. The 1990 industry study that I came across in my research of the Detroit market confirms my assessment of Bea's: "It is extremely poorly run. The décor is nonexistent (essentially, it looks like a high school cafeteria). It is impossible to get a reservation because the phones are unattended during daytime hours."

I made sure All Jokes Aside Detroit was fully staffed to tend to customers' every need, but over at our competition, Bea herself was doing everything. She booked the club. She was at the front door taking the money. She was serving food. I couldn't believe that people went there. I felt like opening All Jokes in Detroit might force her to close up shop. *Wrong.* I have no doubt that she probably made more money than me in Detroit. And if she didn't make more than me, she for damn sure *kept* more than me.

At first, Bea's continued success had me scratching my head. When Detroit audiences came to All Jokes Aside, they could see national headliners for a reasonable admission price of $20. But Bea's only put on local comedians who, though they may have been talented, were pretty much unknown beyond the borders of their hometown. Even from a mere customer service perspective, it was baffling to me that patrons would choose to spend their hard-earned dollars at a hole in the wall when All Jokes offered an upscale alternative at a comparable price. But as Mike pointed out, sometimes people get used to "the same ol' same ol'."

"Everybody doesn't want to go to something elegant," he said. "Sometimes 'upscale' intimidates working-class people. 'Upscale' scares some black folks—'I can't be thug, I can't be 'hood.' Got to put your hat on right and pull your pants up."

With the benefit of 20 years of hindsight, I see the Detroit experience as yet another unintentional lesson in basic black-on-black sociology. In a downwardly mobile place like Detroit, where Motown Records, auto-industry giants, and other corporations had long since abandoned the city's inner core, residents may have felt the need to cling to what was familiar. Even if familiar meant mediocre. That aspect of human behavior may have been especially true for African American consumers, who were used to being taken for granted.

As I saw it, once All Jokes Detroit opened, Bea's shouldn't have even been able to stay open. But there she was, fat and happy. It reminded me of a famous statement by Tony Brown on blacks supporting businesses owned and operated by blacks: "Black folk have committed the greatest economic boycott in the history of American business. Unfortunately, we have conducted it against ourselves."

Mike Bonner summed up his fellow Detroiters' choice of Bea's over All Jokes Aside with a literary analogy: "It was like reading a Donald Goines book as opposed to reading Shakespeare."

We did, however, have a good business in Detroit—and we were growing. We had epic shows, including Laura Hayes, Melanie Comarcho, Carlos Mencia, Tony Woods, and Ricky Harris. Steve Harvey, in particular, flourished there.

"I became a giant in Detroit because of All Jokes Aside," Steve told me when I interviewed him for *Phunny Business*.

Chris Rock considered doing his first HBO special from Detroit because of the audience response that he received while performing at All Jokes Aside. And we did an All Jokes

Aside festival in Detroit as well—four days of sold-out shows featuring the best of the best from around the country.

As fate would have it, in 1996, the city of Detroit reached an agreement with the Detroit Lions and the Detroit Tigers to build new stadiums in the heart of the theater district. Our location sat right in the middle of that area. We would have to move. I was committed to staying in Detroit, and while I loved our location, I saw this as a possibility to reboot the concept. I wanted to stay in the general area, but I figured we could thrive in a smaller venue and create a slim-yet-efficient first-class venue. But first things first: we had to negotiate a deal with the landlord.

My landlord in Detroit, Chuck Forbes, petitioned the city for relief, and about six months later, Chuck reached an agreement regarding all of his properties. This included moving the historic Gem Theatre, which entailed toting the 2,700-ton building to another location four blocks away, at an estimated cost of $1 million. If this 450-seat theater warranted that, I didn't have a problem with it, but I thought I, too, deserved some kind of compensation for All Jokes Detroit being displaced.

Mr. Forbes didn't agree. It was a month-to-month agreement and, thus, he felt that legally he did not have any obligation to me. I disagreed and took my battle to the Detroit City Council. I argued my case before the council and even appeared on TV. I argued that we had established ourselves as a good corporate citizen and a staple in the theater district, and our future was bright. Councilwoman Sheila

Cockrel was a huge supporter and agreed. Many of the pol-
iticians had been to All Jokes Aside and considered us an
important part of the downtown nightlife. They wanted us
to stay. How could Mr. Forbes not agree? He was already a
multimillionaire before this development. How could he not
see that I, too, had an operating business and deserved to be
compensated, just as he had been, so that I could relocate
and continue operations?

In business, sometimes you have to do what's morally right even if you think that you have no legal obligation.
But I had to remind myself once again that my relationship
with Mr. Forbes was based on business—no business, no relationship. After several months of back and forth, I finally
received an embarrassingly low offer from Mr. Forbes, so I
hired a lawyer. It was one of the hardest things that I have
ever had to do in my professional career. I really admired
Mr. Forbes and thought that he felt the same about me.

I filed a lawsuit asserting that everyone affected by this
move had been justly compensated with the exception of
All Jokes Aside. I claimed, as Mr. Forbes himself had been
quoted as saying, that we were a welcome addition to and esteemed member of the theater district. This battle dragged
on for almost a year. Mr. Forbes's lawyers tried to get the
case thrown out, but it didn't work. The judge ruled that I
had a legitimate case. So we began the deposition process,
and it was the first time that I had ever been involved in any
sort of lawsuit, so it was a bit surreal. Being hammered by
$1,000-an-hour lawyers was no fun, but I was angry and up
to the challenge. We were being fucked, and it was simply
not cool. *So hammer away.* I was confident in our claim,

and I felt strongly that if this went to court in Detroit with a jury of my peers, they'd see it that way also. It was a David-versus-Goliath battle if I ever saw one. Hell, the city paid Mr. Forbes $1 million to move the 100-year-old Gem Theatre four blocks. I should be good for at least a million. Right? And it would take that amount, if not a bit more, to relocate and start anew.

It never got that far. After only a few days of depositions, we finally settled with Mr. Forbes, and a closing date and relocation plan were announced.

I spent almost a year after the settlement searching for a suitable location for the club, but I was never able to find one. The theater district was no longer the place for mom-and-pop businesses. The spaces where I could potentially afford the rent would require complete gut renovations. Despite All Jokes's solid business and great reputation, I did not think it wise to spend the time and money investing in such an undertaking. Who knew what impact the stadiums would have? Hell, the venerable Second City closed its doors and left the market, which for me was a sign of things to come. I decided to take a little time to regroup and let the dust settle.

All Jokes Aside Detroit closed its doors in 1997. If circumstances had been different, I could have focused on finding a new location and continued to make a go of it in Detroit. But I had to conserve my energy and resources for another battle that I was facing back home in Chicago.

10
WELCOME TO THE COLORED SECTION

A white woman bakes a chocolate cake. She turns her back, and her li'l boy takes some chocolate and rubs it on his face, says, "Look, Mommy, I'm black." She slaps the shit outta him and says, "Go tell your father what you did!" He goes to his dad, "Look, Daddy, I'm black." He took that belt and beat his ass and said, "Go show your grandfather what you did!" "Look, Grandpa, I'm black." He took a switch out and beat his ass. "Now go back to your mama!" He goes back to his mom, and she says, "Now what did you learn today?" and the little boy says, "I learned that I've been black for five minutes, and I already hate you white mothafuckas."

— PAUL MOONEY

AS THE YEARS WENT ON, I knew that my first entrepreneurial venture was a bona fide success. By 1994, with a whole lot of help from family and friends, All Jokes Aside had grown from a weekend operation run on a shoestring budget to a multimillion-dollar business operating in two of the top comedy markets in America. James and I had even paid back our largest investor—James's mother.

I would say that from 1992 to 1998, I don't think you could have shown me a better room. The only place that would even be close was Carolines in New York. At the height of our success, All Jokes offered 12 shows over five days every week. In the *Phunny Business* documentary, the comedians recalled how it felt to share in our success.

"Turning away a hundred people a night," said George Willborn.

"I'm talking about [lines] down the block," said JB Smoove, "around the corner, around the other corner, and around another corner."

"I couldn't believe it," said Mike Epps. "I'm like, a black man owns this club?"

I was constantly looking for new ways to promote All Jokes Aside and provide a forum for talent. So in 1994, I created a four-day festival that showcased 20 headlining comedians. On any of the four days, festival-goers could take in four 20-minute sets by national headliners.

"Festival Restores Some Respect to Standup," read the headline of an August 1994 story by Allan Johnson for the *Chicago Tribune*. "There was a time when comedy was special," the story said. "This was before free admissions and the resulting diminished respect for the art, a club on almost every street corner, and performers who just a few months before worked in fast-food restaurants. All Jokes Aside, a South Loop comedy club, tried to re-create that time when standup really meant something, with its first comedy festival this past week. Forget that the club's attractions were almost all African American talent. There were some gems to be found for those who love comedy, period."

The All Jokes Aside Comedy Fest was a hit from day one for both the audience and the comedians. For the audience, they were able to see four legitimate headliners in one 90-minute set. For the talent, the festival offered the opportunity to perform in front of a packed house of enthusiastic comedy fans, up close and personal, and alongside their colleagues, the best in the business. It was like the NBA All-Star Game.

Rather than renting a separate venue, we held the festival at the club, which served as another way to promote the All Jokes brand and bring in people who might not otherwise come through our doors. The festival went over so well that audience members often told me they had trouble deciding which day to attend. All of the shows routinely sold out.

As the '90s drew to a close and the new millennium approached, the comedy business began to change. The up-and-comers who got their starts at All Jokes Aside began to pursue lucrative engagements at larger venues.

In their interviews for *Phunny Business*, Bill Bellamy and D.L. Hughley offered their perspectives.

"All the guys who were doing the clubs, honing their craft, became stars," Bill said. "And the guys who became stars started doing theaters."

"People wanted to play concerts and nobody kinda wanted to play comedy clubs," D.L. said.

"So now instead of me playing All Jokes Aside, I was doing the Chicago Theatre, sold out for nights," Bill added. "I was doing the Regal Theater. I was doing [the] Park West [concert hall]."

"It's like a Walmart moving in next to a mom-and-pop store," D.L. said.

Bill summed it up: "For us to be able to make more money doing less shows was the move to make. But what we didn't realize was that we were killing the small guy."

James and I couldn't miss these changes in the industry. Our revenue was essentially flat. We had a solid business, but there had been no growth in several years. We had many heated arguments about the course that we should take. He was completely in favor of producing shows in larger venues. Despite the flat revenue, I saw it as a typical business cycle, and, thus, I wanted to continue with the original vision: a chain of clubs. It would take us longer to build it, but I still thought such a chain could be around for decades, like The Improv and Second City.

James considered starting a subsidiary to do concert-type promotions, which I completely supported; I just didn't want to have anything to do with it. I considered it a different ball game. Being a venue owner and not a concert promoter, I clung to the original All Jokes business model. James never ended up going through with his idea.

I had become a purist. As I saw it, standup comedy belonged in the intimacy of a comedy club. Chris Rock, at his absolute best, in front of 300 enthusiastic fans that get every bit—that's as good as it gets. I didn't see theaters and concert halls as the right venue for comedy, despite the changes happening in the business.

It was small comfort that All Jokes wasn't the only venue affected by the changing comedy industry. As we continued to hold our own, most of the other Chicago clubs closed. Meanwhile, the growth of cable television made the live experience of standup comedy less appealing since audiences could see the same headliners in the comfort of their own homes.

Kelly Leonard, executive vice president of Second City, the legendary Chicago-based improv company, commented on this trend when I interviewed him for *Phunny Business.*

"An interesting thing happened in the mid to late '90s with the standup boom: it went the other way," he said. "And we always theorized it was for a couple different reasons. One was saturation. There was so much standup on TV that was free. Why go to the club?"

While television and concerts ate away at our business, a more potent threat was that the club's location began to make less financial sense. Just as James and I realized that All Jokes's original location at the art gallery cost too much to turn a profit, we eventually came to see that the same was true of the club's "permanent" home at 1000 South Wabash in the South Loop.

By the late '90s, the neighborhood was becoming gentrified, driving up costs and rendering it next to impossible for longtime occupants to stay. The South Loop was becoming a place for big-box stores and chains that could afford to pay astronomical rent. Independent mom-and-pops were on the way out. When I looked critically at the situation, it was simple: rather than facing a typical business cycle, we were at a crossroads, and All Jokes was in trouble. I was facing a 50 percent hike in rent. Comedy concerts and standup all over TV were cutting into our audience. I had to admit that the old business model I was holding on to for dear life was no longer viable. Revenue was flat, and expenses were growing. I had to face a basic business reality: *evolve or die.*

I had an idea. While our business targeting the black market was flat, the general market had gone through a similar cycle a decade earlier but appeared to be ripe for a comeback.

"The *Wall Street Journal* would say we're going through a 'correction,'" said comedian Richard Jeni in a *Los Angeles Times* interview in 1994. "The comedy club experience has been devalued, and there are so many comics around today that you need to be a lot funnier than you needed to be 20 years ago in order to get attention."

In that same article, comedian David Brenner recalled, "There was a club called the Holiday House in Monroeville, Pa., it sat about 1,200, and at one time I would do 10 or 11 nights, two shows a night, and sell it out three weeks before I got to town. Then the club cut down to a six-day week, then just weekends. They went to Friday and Saturday shows only, then just Saturday, then out of business. Now it's a mall."

Chicago was not spared during that period. All of the mainstream clubs in the city, with the exception of Zanies, had closed. At one time, there had been six rooms in the city, including All Jokes Aside, offering a combined 1,500 seats on any given night to see standup. Now, there were only two: All Jokes with 300 seats and Zanies with 100.

So maybe, just maybe, I could go after the entire market: black, white, Latino, and Asian—comedians and audiences of all races. As comedy legend George Carlin said, "Everyone smiles in the same language."

Moreover, I had worked with all of the major comedy talent agencies and management companies, so I could book any comic I wanted who was still working clubs. And there were hundreds of them. They called me daily.

This, however, would require closing All Jokes Aside. The brand was so entrenched in the black community that if I were to offer anything other that what I had been doing, it would have been seen as abandonment. As black entrepreneurs, we often carry the weight of not just being good businessmen and businesswomen; we also carry the weight of the people. I couldn't just be an entrepreneur; I was a *black* entrepreneur with a social agenda as well. I had no problem with that; in fact, I welcomed it, but there are times when you have to be a businessperson, pure and simple. If I wanted to make this move, I'd have to shut down the existing club and start a new concept. That's what I decided to do. And with a very heavy heart, that is just what I did. All Jokes Aside's Wabash Avenue location closed in August 1998. This left the venerable Zanies in Old Town as Chicago's only full-time comedy club.

As I did in the early days when moving All Jokes Aside to the new permanent space, I kept my plan a secret. I was working alone. Mary had already moved on to pursue another venture, and James had accepted a buyout. While this was the final curtain on All Jokes Aside, the closing of the Wabash location was a prelude to a new beginning. Or so I thought.

Once I had decided on a concept, I began to look around at different business models and different businesses. I wanted this venue to be less like Budd Friedman's The Improv and more like Caroline Hirsch's Carolines in New York City. But

I didn't confine myself to studying only companies in my direct industry. I did market research on all types of companies, looking for ones that exemplified excellence, ones that I could learn from and use as models. Although I was in the comedy-club business operationally, I planned to model myself after Zingerman's Delicatessen of Ann Arbor, Michigan.

As I did with Houston's in the early days of All Jokes Aside, I studied up on Zingerman's. I read an article about it in *Inc.* magazine titled "The Coolest Small Company in America," which asked, "Why are high-powered MBA's getting off the fast track to work for a $13 million food company in Ann Arbor?"

That's what I wanted my business to be: one location that would become nationally celebrated. My dream was that the new venue would be lauded as the best comedy club in America.

With only Zanies to compete with, I decided to locate my club just a mile and a half north of the All Jokes location, closer to the heart of the city's mainstream entertainment district. No doubt, the demographic that I had been serving was the African American market. I believed All Jokes had come to represent African American excellence and had evolved into an important part of Chicago's black community. This was my chance to establish All Jokes in the general market as well as re-establish myself with the remaining All Jokes supporters. It would be the best of both worlds. Even so, there were those who felt it just wouldn't be the same. "There was a spirit of black comedy that existed in All Jokes Aside," comedian Don "DC" Curry said during our *Phunny Business* interview, "and I think some of that is lost when you 'upgrade.'"

I came up with an idea for a new venue that I would call Monologue. I decided on a new name in part because it seemed to make sense for a new location. And besides, the All Jokes Aside brand had become synonymous with African American comedy, and the new venue would feature not only the best from All Jokes Aside but also the best of the rest. I would have something for everybody—and I'd be the only comedy club in a city of 3 million people doing that. I wanted Monologue to be more than a comedy club. I wanted it to encompass a restaurant, a lounge where customers could relax and hang out, and a comedy spot with "the All Jokes Aside Stage" to honor the legacy of the original club. As a customer, I envisioned you could spend three hours in there and have three different experiences.

The first step in realizing this new vision was to find a new location. And I did just that at 108 West Kinzie Street. Derrel McDavid, one of R. Kelly's managers, owned the building. McDavid was a family friend of my dear friend Kim Porter. Derrel had an office in the South Loop, and he understood that my goal for Monologue was to entertain the masses, just like the world-famous R&B singer he managed. R. Kelly had been to All Jokes Aside on several occasions, and Derrel definitely got it.

Chicago's River North neighborhood was and is one of the most thriving entertainment districts in the entire United States. Despite its upscale surroundings, the building I found for Monologue was in need of a major facelift. Like in the corny old adage about real estate, it was the worst house on the best block. Traffic in the area was no better. But the rent was only 25 percent more than it was at our Wabash location.

But first things first: in Chicago, it is "traditional," and smart, that before you start any project, you pay your respects to the alderman of that ward. So before I signed the lease and began renovations, I sought the endorsement of Alderman Burton Natarus, a legendary figure in Chicago politics.

My attorney at the time, Kevin Freeman, made the appointment, and that first meeting with Alderman Natarus couldn't have gone better. He told me he thought Monologue would be a great addition to the ward. He was aware of us, and he knew that All Jokes Aside's South Loop location had never had a brush with the law or problems of any sort in eight years of operation.

For about a decade, River North had been home to two major comedy clubs, The Improv and The Funny Firm. Both were 400-seat clubs that featured top national headliners like Bill Hicks, Bill Maher, Sam Kinison, Bobcat Goldthwait, Janeane Garofalo, Rosie O'Donnell, Louis C.K., and a host of others. I was a frequent visitor at both clubs, which were located two blocks from each other and only a few blocks from my new location. Both had closed around '94 or '95, so my hope was that my new club would fill that void.

After the encouraging meeting with Alderman Natarus, I signed the lease on the space and hired one of the city's hottest young architects. Obi Nwazota—a Nigerian who was educated in London—drew up plans to redesign the space and realize the setup I had in mind. What Obi and I were trying to create was a versatile entertainment venue, a place for comedy, cocktails, dining, and conversation.

With this full-service concept in mind, I approached the well-known restaurateurs Tom and Dino Bezanes to design the menu. I had known Tom and Dino from their restaurant Standing Room Only in the South Loop. I was a regular and a big fan. Born and raised in Chicago, the Bezanes brothers knew the restaurant business in and out, and, most importantly, they were excellent operators. The vision they had for the restaurant portion of Monologue was in sync with mine, and I was excited about having them as partners. Tom and Dino agreed and signed on to the new venture.

With the architect and restaurant team on board, everything was all systems go. We secured our building permits and began construction. I even hired a public relations firm to plan the launch. Monologue seemed to be on track to become a reality.

But as the saying goes, sometimes the best laid plans . . . .

In an April 14, 2000, *Chicago Tribune* article headlined "Another Chance to Get a Laugh in Chicago," journalists Ellen Warren, Terry Armour, and Allan Johnson described my new venture:

"We can all use a laugh, so this has got to be good news. A full-time comedy club is opening here at the end of the month—bringing the grand total of such Chicago spots to . . . two. Ever since the boom of the '80s, the city's comedy scene has been on the decline, with 'for rent' signs popping up in all the places we used to go for a yuk or two. Now comes Monologue, opening April 28 at 108 W. Kinzie St. in River North. Currently, only Zanies on Wells Street is all-comedy."

In a June 3, 2000, article on *Metromix Chicago*, journalist Audarshia Townsend wrote: "Is it cunning or simply by chance that three of Chicago's most revered and cutting-edge club owners are resurfacing in the year 2000?

"The 1990s belonged to Barry Paddor of Shelter, Calvin Hollins of the Clique and Raymond Lambert of All Jokes Aside. For Hollins and Lambert, it was a matter of shaping Chicago's black nightlife. Hollins' flashy Clique brought in the heavy hitters of urban music, from Puff Daddy to Mariah Carey, while Lambert's All Jokes attracted high-profile comics like Steve Harvey and Sinbad. When both closed, the loss was devastating.

"The recent openings of multimillion dollar E2 Chicago (Hollins) and colorfully hip Monologue (Lambert) promise to breathe life back into local black nightlife. And most certainly they will be offering patrons breathtaking atmospheres as well as high-quality entertainment."

While the positive press was gratifying, the good cheer didn't last long. I wish I could say I was surprised when I heard from our contractor, who happened to be white, that my new neighbors, the owners of the art galleries and antique shops, were going to file a petition to keep me from getting my liquor license. Monologue couldn't exist without a liquor license. I had selected that location because it was commercial. There were at least a half-dozen bars on the same block. I had met with many of the local business owners individually. I thought they liked me. Everybody loves Raymond, right?

I sought advice from Alderman Natarus, who had initially seemed to offer his full support. But ultimately, he had to bend to the will of his constituents. And anyone who knows anything about Chicago politics knows that it can get messy.

Real messy. And doing business in the Windy City can be costly. It's not so much that raw materials and labor are expensive; it's that navigating the choppy waters of Chicago's notorious political machine to obtain licenses and permits is a dicey endeavor. This process can potentially bankrupt almost any business, especially a new one that's struggling to get on its feet.

I thought maybe Dino Bezanes and his crew, who had experience working in restaurants in the River North district, could intervene on my behalf. After speaking to some people who represented the alderman at the time, Dino told me they said something to the effect of, "The economic status of the clientele is not conducive to the neighborhood." So he asked them point blank, "So what you're trying to say is, you don't want any black people?"

Since River North was an entertainment district zoned for commercial use and All Jokes Aside had an impeccable eight-year license history at its Wabash Avenue location, the liquor license for Monologue should have been a done deal. But the way the system was set up, one person could object to a license and the applicant would have to defend his right to exist.

According to the complaint, my neighbors-to-be argued that Monologue, as planned, would, and I quote, "change the tone of the block," "change the ambiance of the neighborhood," "culturally threaten their enclave," and "have a deleterious impact on the community."

Mind you, this same neighborhood has an adult bookstore, a porn shop, and a club with female impersonators.

By the time my so-called "neighbors" filed their appeal in August 1999, I had invested nearly $1 million in trying to open

Monologue. With that kind of money on the table, I wasn't going down without a fight. I had faced similar obstacles in Washington and Detroit, and now I was facing this, in a city where I had earned a stellar reputation. Whatever the objectors' problems were, this was going to have to play itself out in court. And quickly, I hoped. I was almost out of money.

Preparing for battle, I lawyered up. I also reached out to my former alderman, Ted Mazola, as well as Dorothy Tillman, a well-known and well-connected African American alderman who I knew was a big fan of All Jokes Aside. I had heard Alderman Tillman was developing a well-funded entertainment district in her South Side ward, an area that, at the time, was in much need of redevelopment. The area had been designated a tax increment financing district (TIF), which is a special funding tool used by the City of Chicago to promote public and private investments across the city.

At one time, Alderman Tillman's ward encompassed the Bronzeville neighborhood that was the entertainment hub for Chicago's black community. All the big stars played on 47th Street, as far back as Louis Armstrong and up through Duke Ellington, Nat King Cole, Dinah Washington, Lou Rawls, and on and on. But beginning in the '70s, the ward lost its way, and all of its great venues closed. I believe in hoping for the best but preparing for the worst. I figured that if I lost this North Side battle with the petitioners, there might be an opportunity for me in Alderman Tillman's ward.

Timing had worked in my favor when James and I first opened All Jokes and rode the wave of the early '90s comedy boom. But as the century drew to a close, the timing was against me, and the opposing forces seemed to snowball.

As it turned out, I was a bit too late in approaching Alderman Tillman. Andrew Alexander, CEO and co-owner of Second City, had beaten me to the punch. Alexander (no relation to James) had contacted Alderman Tillman because he wanted to expand Second City's diversity efforts and provide a forum to showcase African American improv performers. Alderman Tillman may have been a fan and frequent customer at All Jokes Aside, but she was seduced by the prospect of a "Black Second City." The way I saw it, Second City and Monologue could coexist in Bronzeville. Both of our organizations had served as launching pads for countless comedy stars.

I have a tremendous amount of respect for Second City. I aspired to its level of excellence. It was sheer coincidence that both the Second City folks and I were planning new incarnations of our brands. As far as I was concerned, it didn't have to be an "us against them" situation. Second City is a sketch comedy house; Monologue would have been standup. I felt there was room for both.

In fact, I had actually collaborated years before with the Second City folks. Andrew Alexander and Kelly Leonard had contacted me in the mid '90s to discuss how All Jokes Aside could help Second City diversify its talent roster. Andrew's idea was that when headline-grabbing events like the 1992 Los Angeles riots broke out, an all-white cast shouldn't try to interpret such polarizing events.

During that time, I had lunch with Kelly and started talking about the things that Second City wanted to do and how that might enhance what we had going on at All Jokes Aside. The meeting was a friendly brainstorming session among peers who sought to complement one another, not steal business from each other. Kelly told me they weren't interested in being the "Big Bad White Wolf." Ultimately, Second City assembled a troupe of actors of color who occasionally performed at All Jokes. After this successful collaboration, I stayed in touch with the Second City folks over the years.

But looking back now, all I can do is shake my head, reflecting on what could have been but never was. The combined forces of Second City and the new Monologue could have created a comedy megaplex in Bronzeville and bolstered Chicago's reputation as a training ground for comedians of all races. We could have created a whole comedy scene. Zanies is literally a block south of Second City. They've survived a block away from each other for 30 years. Why couldn't we have done the same thing on the South Side? Instead of the City of Chicago giving Second City $2.4 million in TIF funding, why not give them $1.4 million and give me the rest?

As relocating to the new Bronzeville entertainment district was no longer a possibility, I had no choice but to focus my energy on the long, drawn-out River North fight. I think it was June of 2000 when I got the call from my lawyer that the verdict was in.

I won.

However, I was done. The court battle had dragged on month after month, draining resources I otherwise would have been investing in the business. After two years of fighting, I had run out of time, money, and energy. I took one last look around the site I had intended for Monologue, put the keys on the bar, and walked out the door.

I had 32 cents in my bank account.

Folks often say to me, *Why didn't you just pay off the powers that be—the Chicago way?* I wish it had been that easy. Even ignoring the fact that I tried to play by the rules, from a practical standpoint, I simply couldn't do it. In these United States, one thing a black man can never depend on is getting the benefit of the doubt. The game is just not set up that way. Honest John, who happens to be white and one of my favorite comedians, puts it this way: "Do you know why black people don't play hockey? If a white boy checks someone hard against the glass, he gets 7–10 minutes in the penalty box. If a brother did the same exact thing, he'd get 7–10 years in prison for assault and battery."

I can see it now: "And now with local news: Raymond Lambert, owner of the popular comedy club All Jokes Aside, an intelligent, well-educated, and accomplished young man, was caught today by undercover agents attempting to bribe a city official to get a liquor license. The all-white jury deliberated for 15 minutes, and Lambert was sentenced to 12 years in prison. One would think that if he had just continued to work hard, play by the rules, and wait his turn, he could have been successful. What a fall from grace. Now here's Paul with the weather."

I couldn't do business as "usual." Not to mention that I've been inside a jail cell, and I know it's not a good look. One thing that I know for sure—because I watched *Oz* on HBO—I'm too small, too handsome, and too recalcitrant to do well in jail. I would not last a week. I try to stay away from situations where I cannot do well. My intentions are to never do anything that I could potentially go to jail for. Period.

In the end, I had lost a lot more than money. What hurt the most was that my dad had invested $50,000—half of his life savings. I felt like a deadbeat, an idiot, an incompetent fool.

In a painful twist, a white-owned establishment ended up moving into the space I had planned for Monologue. No complaints were filed. No petitions sought. Interestingly, the white-owned business lasted for only a few years before they closed after having a few issues with the law. Issues my would-be neighbors were so afraid that my business would have brought to the area.

And the "Black Second City" that had courted Alderman Tillman and Bronzeville? It never materialized.

My dream of a new, full-service entertainment venue in a gleaming facility situated in a bustling entertainment district that was ideal for catering to people of all races would remain just that—a dream.

When viewed through the lens of history, the racism I encountered when trying to open Monologue in River North wasn't surprising. Dr. Martin Luther King once described Chicago as America's most segregated city.

"Chicago has a long and proud history of being racist," Ernest Tucker, a comedian and former writer for the *Chicago Sun-Times*, said during an interview for *Phunny Business*. "That's not me making this up or coming to some grand conclusion."

African Americans outnumber any other ethnic group in Chicago, according to a 2009 demographic study by real estate research firm The Chicago 77. Of the city's nearly 3 million people, 35 percent are African American, 30 percent are Hispanic, and 28 percent are white. But despite apparent strength in numbers, "blacks in Chicago are the most isolated racial group in the nation's 20 largest cities," *Chicago Tribune* journalists Azam Ahmed and Darnell Little wrote in a December 2008 article. "To truly integrate Chicago, 84 percent of the black or white population would need to change neighborhoods."

It seems that not much has changed in the five decades since Dr. King's observation. The Chicago 77 did a demographic study in 2009 that confirmed segregation was still alive and well in the Windy City, even after the nation elected the first African American president—a president who got his start in Chicago politics and maintains deep ties to the city.

11

A PATH APPEARS

I'm not delusional. I'm an entrepreneur. —HUGH MACLEOD

THERE COMES A TIME in the life of every entrepreneur where they reach that fork in the road: *Is this just another obstacle to be overcome or a sign to let go of your dreams? When do you keep going versus when should you just quit? And how do you know?*

The experience of trying to open Monologue discouraged me greatly. I had been beaten down, rejected, and lied to, plus I had lost all that I had built with All Jokes Aside and disappointed many of my staunchest supporters. *Is this it?*, I wondered. *Had my dreams of being a self-made man come to an end? Was the promise I had shown as a younger man a thing of the past? Was it time to finally get a "real" job?*

When it became clear that I wasn't going to be able to open Monologue as planned, I tried to stay positive. I started reading Paulo Coelho's classic inspirational book *The Alchemist,* and every week, I chanted, "In pursuing your dreams, you might lose everything that you've won." I tried to take this insight to heart and keep things in perspective, but there was still that cloud hanging over me. I had personally guaranteed the loans for Monologue. There was still the landlord and vendors to pay in excess of $250,000, which I fully intended to repay, somehow. And I didn't have any prospects of generating income.

Depressed, I took a year to mull things over. I had just gotten married, and my then wife, Schnell Price, understood what I was going through. But our first daughter, Nia Rae, was on the way. So I decided to take the Monologue experience as a sign, not an obstacle, and abandon my lifelong dream of being an entrepreneur. I returned to a day job.

What's so great about entrepreneurship, anyway? Working for yourself is overrated, I reasoned. Contrary to what most people think, entrepreneurship isn't all it's cracked up to be. In his book, *The Illusions of Entrepreneurship*, Scott Shane points out that much of what we think we know about entrepreneurship is based on myths. People think that the typical entrepreneur is a jet-setting, Silicon Valley–residing engineer who, along with a couple of his buddies, has raised millions of dollars of venture capital to start a new company to make a patent-protected gizmo. This hot new startup will, of course, employ thousands of people, go public in four years, and generate huge gobs of money for its founders and investors.

Not so.

According to Shane, the typical entrepreneur in America is a married white man in his 40s who attended but did not complete college. He lives in a place like Des Moines or

Tampa, where he was born and has lived much of his life. His new business is a low-tech endeavor in an industry where he has worked for years—most likely before he was laid off. The typical new business is a sole proprietorship, financed with $25,000 of the founder's savings and maybe a bank loan that he personally guaranteed. The average entrepreneur has no plans to employ lots of people or to make a lot of money. He is just trying to earn a living and support his family.

And for the typical black entrepreneur, it's an even more precarious situation. Shane states that the performance of black-owned startups is much worse than that of white-owned ones, according to virtually every measurable dimension: long-term survival, sales, profits, employment, and so on. But the primary reason that black-led startups perform worse than white-led startups is that they are undercapitalized. A 2009 survey of Chicago businesses found that 63 percent of black firm owners had a difficult time obtaining sufficient working capital—the highest percentage among all racial groups. I can personally attest to those struggles.

I opted to to become an *intra-preneur*: someone who acts like an entrepreneur while working within a large organization. I no longer wanted to have to worry about the light bill, motivate minimum-wage employees, or find customers, bankers, vendors, investors, and comedians. I simply wanted to show up, do my job well, go home, and play with my kids. Done.

My only limitation was that my wife, Schnell, was entrenched in a family business based in Milwaukee. So I could not, in good conscience, leave and take a high-paying job on either coast, where I had great contacts. I could travel, but work-wise, I had to make it happen while remaining based in Chicago.

I had been offered opportunities to become an agent or manager, but I had no interest in that. I just did not have the nurturing personality or patience to succeed at it. I liked running businesses. Having worked closely with producers at HBO, Comedy Central, and BET, I had developed a strong interest in cable television. In addition, I had produced my own hour of television for the local NBC affiliate. At the dawn of the 2000s, cable was where the progressive programming was happening. It seemed rife with opportunity.

At the time, it perplexed me that with more than 35 million black folk in America, there was only one network—BET—targeting the black market. After all, I had been programing 12 shows a week at All Jokes Aside for a decade. I had a history of entering businesses in which I had no direct experience. I figured if it had been done before, I could do it. I began looking for a job at a network.

My good friend Susan Scott introduced me to a few folks at USA Network and Starz Entertainment. As corporations go, they both appeared very open to me being an "intra-preneur," but Starz was especially appealing to me on several levels. One, it was a subscriber-based network. That's where the action and growth was. Two, the position available to me was very similar to the role I held at Coca-Cola. Three, cable overall was still a relatively young industry, and Starz Entertainment Group was an up-and-comer.

John Malone, one of the cable industry's pioneer legends, owned Starz. John Sie, the president of the company, was a cable pioneer as well, and they had built Starz into the third-largest pay service behind HBO and Showtime. When the opportunity to work for the Chicago-based division of Starz came up, I jumped at it.

Management expressed a strong interest in my background, as they wanted to be more entrepreneurial. While I was overqualified for the position that I was offered—my direct manager did not have a college degree, and MBAs were rare at the company—I didn't care. I just wanted in. I had no problem with starting from scratch. Moreover, the company was growing fast, and all that I had ever wanted was to rise as fast and as high as my talent and ability would take me. Hell, I was content to have a paycheck every two weeks, great benefits, a matching 401(k) plan, and a nice office—and not have to pay for them myself.

Once I was settled in, I called my father to tell him the good news about my new job. We didn't talk often, maybe once a month at most. But I was also trying to refinish my deck, and he knew everything there is to know about wood. He had a full-service woodshop in his basement, organized to the hilt. It was late February, the weather was breaking, and I was preparing to tackle the deck on the first good day of spring. I was calling to ask about what products I should buy.

During that conversation, which as fate would have it, would be our last, I mentioned that there was a Home Depot right down the street where I could purchase sealant and rent the equipment to do the job. But I wanted to talk to him first.

My dad was not a fan of Home Depot. He said, "Man, fuck Home Depot, overpriced motherfuckers. Go to Ace Hardware, and get their brand. That shit is good, and they will rent you the equipment at a hip price. Fuck Home Depot."

I laughed out loud. The shit my dad says! He used to talk to me like that back when I was just a five-year-old kid. I come from a family of master cursers. As a kid, I thought that was just how people talked to each other—right up until I went to school. I bet my kindergarten teacher still remembers me for that: "Mrs. Thomas, would you please tell Bobby to give me my mothafuckin' crayons?" I didn't know.

Some time later, I called my dad again to tell him I had gotten the stuff and it had worked well. More importantly, I wanted to schedule a time for him to come visit his first granddaughter, Nia Rae. She was a few months old and he had yet to meet her. Right around June 10, on the birthday I shared with my father, seemed liked the perfect time to plan for him to come to Chicago. The weather would have broken, and Nia would be six months by then and ready for him.

When I called my dad, I was surprised when my uncle Harold answered the phone. He didn't recognize my voice at first, and I had to tell him it was me. The call went something like this:

ME:
Hello, who's this?

UNCLE HAROLD:
This is Harold, who's this?

ME:
Courtney [my middle name, which my family still calls me].
Uncle Harold, how are you?

UNCLE HAROLD:
Your father's dead.

ME:
What?

UNCLE HAROLD:
Your father's dead.

ME:
What do you mean, my father's dead?

UNCLE HAROLD:
We found him in the basement this morning.
The police are here.

ME:
What do you mean, you found him?

UNCLE HAROLD:
We don't know what happened. When can you get here?

ME:
I just talked to him. He was supposed to meet
Nia in a few months.

UNCLE HAROLD:
I'm sorry. I wish he could have met her.

ME:
Goddammit . . . me too. I'm on my way.

It was the most surreal thing that has ever happened to
me. My dad was just 60. We had reached a really comfortable

place. A few months earlier, for the first time in my life, he had told me that he was proud of me. I was 40, but it was cool, nonetheless. Perhaps he knew the end was near and wanted me to know that. All kids, no matter how old, want their parents to be proud of them.

I discovered later that Dad had been deeply depressed. He had just gone through his second divorce. During that process, and unbeknownst to me and my brother, he had been diagnosed as bipolar. Albeit too late, the diagnosis was a revelation, and it explained a lot about his behavior during my childhood. It was a relief. But his death and the mystery surrounding it was a punch in the gut. *Could it be suicide? No way. Black men don't kill themselves. That's white people shit. We survived slavery.* It was like I was floating on a cloud.

After that call with Uncle Harold, I walked out of my office at Starz without saying a word. I could not speak. I ran home, in my work clothes, five miles away. It took me an hour and a half. Over the years, I had become a marathon runner, and running had become my way to escape the world. I am good at compartmentalizing—it has something to do with my self-diagnosed touch of attention deficit disorder.

By the time I got home, I had gathered myself. I told Schnell that my father had died and I had to go to Wilmington. I packed a bag, called my travel agent on the way to the airport, and I was in Wilmington by dinnertime.

As I made funeral preparations and provisions for all of Dad's belongings—he was a major pack rat—I was just going through the motions. I was being the man I was supposed to be in these sorts of situations, but I was in real pain.

I worked closely with the funeral home. My brother, Nevan, and I picked out his clothes, made the program, spoke to the church and extended family. Even then, I thought, *This ain't real. He's going to come in here at any moment and say something only my dad would say. Something like, "I was just fucking with y'all."*

It was not "real" until the day before the funeral, when we had to view the body. That's when I lost it. My mother refused to attend the services, and I did not plead with her to do so. It wouldn't have helped anyway. As my aunts would say, "You laid him out nice." I never inquired as to the cause of death; it didn't matter. He was gone. He would never meet Nia Rae. I wished he could have met her.

At Starz, I became a district manager of affiliate relations, and in that role, I led and managed Starz's relationship with the Time Warner Cable and Charter Communications accounts in the Great Lakes division. The area I was assigned encompassed 1 million cable television subscribers. Starz was a first-class operation, and they were very generous with their staff. During my first few months on the job, we had a meeting in Denver that included an excursion to the ski slopes in Breckenridge.

Even during the heyday of All Jokes Aside, I never had all of the resources that I needed in order to be the absolute best that I could be. I just did the best that I could with what I had. In contrast, working at Starz was great. I had everything that I could possibly need to produce results. And I did. I led a direct team of three professionals and an indirect team of 12, and I managed an annual budget of about $8 million. I was charged with developing and executing a strategic sales and marketing plan to drive analog and digital subscriber growth.

And I enjoyed it. I was comfortable. It was nice walking into an office and not worrying about anything but the job that I was charged with. No comedians, no staff, and somebody else to pay the light bill. I was able to increase the subscriber base by an average of 25 percent annually and grow revenue by an average of 17 percent annually in the five years I was at Starz. Life was good.

I came to grips with my dad's death. I negotiated and settled with all of my debtors from my Monologue days. Nia Rae was the light of life, and Schnell was pregnant with our second child, Maya Jo. And then it happened.

Approaching my fifth year with the company, Starz decided to consolidate, close its Chicago office, and move the operations to Denver. I briefly thought about relocating, but with all due respect, by that point, the only city that I wanted to live and work in was Chicago. I was locked in. I had a small child and another on the way to consider, and my wife traveled to Milwaukee twice a week for her family's business. So I was not going anywhere. And to be honest, while I loved the comforts of corporate life, I had to admit that I was not content.

Deep in the inner recesses of my soul, the dream of being a successful entrepreneur would not die. Yet the day-to-day grind of that life had lost all appeal. How could I combine the security and comforts of corporate life with the creativity and independence of being an entrepreneur? How could I find the best of both worlds?

One day, I read an article in *Businessweek* on the severe shortage of business school professors in entrepreneurship. *That's it!* I could already see it: *Dr. Raymond Lambert, distinguished professor of entrepreneurship. Scholar, researcher, strategic consultant.*

I had always wanted to teach, but I had never seriously thought about being a full-time professor. It sounded great, and I had actual entrepreneurial experience. I had found my new calling.

I began the process of researching programs and came across one that seemed perfect: The PhD Project. The PhD Project is a catalyst for African Americans, Hispanic Americans, and Native Americans to return to academia to earn doctorates and become business professors.

I immediately applied to the program and was accepted. I learned, however, that my acceptance was the exception. At 44, I was considered old. Most PhD students enter a program immediately after undergrad and by the time they are 40, they are tenured professors. But my interest was in an emerging area of study, and entrepreneurship was a hot topic. My background made me uniquely qualified for the program.

I was truly excited. I attended the conference full of optimism and met admissions officers from all of the top schools, including Harvard, Wharton, Booth, Columbia, Northwestern, Virginia, Duke, and a host of others. But I was only interested in one school: Harvard. As with business school, I loved its case method of study, and this time, I was not intimidated by Harvard's history and stature.

I called everyone I knew who had attended or taught at Harvard Business School, as well as anyone else who was connected to the school in any way. One of my first calls was to Steven Rogers, a Harvard Business School graduate who was then the head of the Entrepreneurship Program at Northwestern University's Kellogg School of Management. Steven had been a big fan of All Jokes Aside, and I regularly spoke to his classes about entrepreneurship. His students and I had written a business school case about All Jokes Aside. He didn't think I needed a PhD. He didn't have one himself. But he understood my desire to pursue it and promised to support me in any way that he could.

My next call was to Tommy Amaker, Harvard's head basketball coach. I had met Tommy on a flight, and he was best friends with Teddy Carpenter, a comedian whom I regularly booked at All Jokes. I had a great relationship with Teddy, and Tommy and I got along well.

I also called a few Morehouse alumni and professors from Darden who had completed The PhD Project. I received support from all.

I went to the Harvard campus, sat in on a few classes, and was convinced that it was the place for me. I began the process in earnest. I planned to commute and work year-round to complete the program in four years or less—a feat, to be sure, but it had been done before. I would take the severance package from Starz, take a year off to study for the entrance exams, and prepare to once again be a student.

Then my brother called. "You need to get home," Nevan said. "Mom is not doing well."

After his basic training in the Navy Reserve, Nevan had returned to Wilmington and was working in credit card billing and processing operations with Chase.

My mother had suffered a multitude of health issues for practically her whole life, primarily as a result of her alcoholism. These included diabetes and acute respiratory distress syndrome. She had been doing well, but it had all caught up with her. The doctors were doing what they could but were not optimistic. She had spent a month in the intensive care unit, and I had been commuting a few days weekly from Chicago to Wilmington to give my brother a break and to care for her. She was being kept alive by machines.

When I arrived in Chicago after Nevan's call, the doctors informed us that they had done all that they could. It was in our best interest to allow her to die.

My mother never wanted to live via machines, and my brother and I decided to take her off life support. They expected her to die within hours of being removed from the machines, but in true Patterson form, she proved to be a fighter. After two days of her breathing on her own, we moved her to hospice.

Initially, hospice was a scary place for me. The inevitability of it all was emotionally taxing. Moreover, I did not want to be in the room when she took her last breath. I just didn't think that I could handle it. But one day while I was visiting, one of the nurses pulled me to the side and she said something that got me through the whole ordeal.

She said, "Were you in the room when your kids were born?"

I said, "Yes."

"Both of them?"

"Yes."

"You must know that just as there is honor in birth, there is honor in death."

Thank you.

I decided to stay with my mother around the clock. And like old folks used to do when someone was dying, I cracked the window so that her soul could escape when the time came.

One morning after being there through the night, the nurse told me to go home, take a shower, get a few hours' sleep, and come back after breakfast. I was asleep for about 30 minutes when the call came. My mother had died. I should have been there. I had been there the past few days for 24 hours straight. The nurse must have heard the shame in my voice.

She told me over the phone, "Don't feel bad about not being by her side. Your mother did not want you to see her take her last breath. She waited until you left."

I ran to where she was in the hospice to find they had cleaned her up nicely. She looked like she was simply taking a nap. What was distinctive was how cold her body was. I had just kissed her on the forehead two hours before, and she had been burning up. My dad's death was like someone reached into my chest and pulled my heart out. My mother's death felt like they reached in, pulled it out again, and stomped on it.

We buried her a week later at the same cemetery as her parents and my dad but on opposite sides of the lawn. They fought like cats and dogs in real life, and I would be damned if they were going to fight in the afterlife.

In a three-month period, I had gone from the high of the birth of my second child to the low of the death of my mother. And right after burying my father. It was hard to focus, but I returned to Chicago and continued to prepare for my exams.

One day, while I was at home studying, I got a call from John Davies, an independent producer based in LA, inquiring if I'd be interested in a comedy festival that he and his partner, Jason Bruce, were putting together. I had known of John from my days with All Jokes Aside and from working with Bob Zmuda, the president of Comic Relief. I had worked with Bob and the late Andy Kaufman's family for several years, producing a Christmas show benefiting homeless children that was held at All Jokes. Our first show featured Sinbad and Vanna White. Vanna did not do standup; she was one of the many celebrities that supported Comic Relief. Apparently, she wears those gowns everywhere.

When I first started working at Starz, I introduced John to our programming team. He was pitching an idea based on the book *Spinning Blues into Gold*, but at the time, Starz was only doing specials, and they didn't feel that it was a good fit. But the comedy festival John and Jason were putting together sounded like a good idea. I had done a festival at the club for years, and Chicago was a great market in which to try it on a larger scale.

John and Jason were going to kick off their festival with a tribute to Chicago's rich comedy history, and they wanted to feature All Jokes Aside as a part of it. I understood that I represented the "black" component of this history, but I didn't care. I was proud of what we created, and I knew that I could put together a showcase that would be the talk of the festival. So I was cool with it. It's not how you start; it's how you finish.

Working on the festival gave me something to do in addition to studying for exams. We met several times, but John and Jason ultimately decided not to do it. As it turned out, Just For Laughs, a Montreal-based festival producer, had announced plans to bring a version of its world-renowned festival to Chicago. Just For Laughs produces the largest comedy festival in the world. I had consulted with them for several years, and they were a world-class organization. John and Jason retreated.

In the midst of this planning, we were talking over beers one night, and John asked what had really happened to All Jokes. The more we talked about it, the more it became clear that there was a story to tell. John broached the idea of creating a documentary film that told the All Jokes story. I had never considered a documentary; I always saw the story as a narrative feature film, but the more I thought about it, the more it made sense.

John and I began to do a bit of research and discovered that there had been several docs made about comedy venues, but one in particular that convinced me that we, too, had a story to tell was a film called *When Stand Up Stood Out*, which chronicles the explosive popularity of the Boston standup comedy scene in the '80s and early '90s. The film includes interviews with many comedians who got their start in Boston, such as Kevin Meaney, Denis Leary, Steven Wright, Janeane Garofalo, Bobcat Goldthwait, Paula Poundstone, and Lenny Clarke, to name a few.

After watching the film, John asked if I had a list of all of the headliners that I had booked over the years. I did, and when I looked at the roster of comics, it was overwhelming.

Until that point, I may never have looked at the entire roster of All Jokes performers at one time.

"Let's do it," I told John. If *When Stand Up Stood Out* could do it with that roster, then I felt confident about the All Jokes roster, which was just as strong, if not stronger.

My film credits to that point had been my work as associate producer on the movie *Slow Burn*, which was written and directed by Wayne Beach. I had sold the idea to Wayne, and he ran with it. I got to visit the set in Montreal and meet Ray Liotta, LL Cool J, Taye Diggs, and Mekhi Phifer. I also met the lesser-known Chiwetel Ejiofor, the star of that film, who, of course, went on to be nominated for the Best Actor Oscar in 2014 for *12 Years a Slave*. I had a great time and vowed to one day produce a film of my own—from start to finish.

John enlisted the help of Reid Brody, a Chicago-based producer. As president of Filmworkers Collective, a post-production film company, Reid had an extensive background in video post production and was making a move into the producing side of filmmaking. Reid had just finished making the movie *Nothing Like the Holidays* and was all in for the All Jokes Aside documentary. He had office space and an editing suite and a staff to assist in the post-production process.

John recommended that we use a young cinematographer/editor named Brian Kallies. Brian was a Chicago guy whom John had worked with and a cat who was eager to build his résumé. I began to call a few comedians to get a feel for whether they were game and willing to participate gratis. We did not have the budget to pay for interviews and we didn't want to bring on investors. We decided to do it ourselves, and I wrote the first check to get us started.

From day one, it was a labor of love. But it wasn't fun. Making a film is very hard, taxing work. It is not glamorous at all. I liken it to running a marathon. It's rewarding in the end but not in the traditional "fun" kind of experience. Overall, however, it was plenty gratifying to set a goal, work hard at it, and finish strong.

One year turned into two, and two turned into three. My dream of earning my PhD and becoming a business school professor were put on the back burner as I pursued the film. This was my opportunity to produce a full movie, and most importantly, it was *my* story.

The comics were gracious and very giving of their time and energy. More than two dozen comedians and a dozen supporters of the club were interviewed. I got to personally interview Steve Harvey, Carlos Mencia, D.L. Hughley, Deon Cole, George Willborn, and Doug Banks, to name a few. I was at every other interview with the exception of two, and I was in the editing suite every day. It was film school 101. I commissioned new music, and I even worked with the graphic artist on the original website design and movie poster. I participated in every aspect of the process. I really dug that.

All of the work paid off. The film, titled *Phunny Business: A Black Comedy*, premiered at the Santa Barbara International Film Festival to rave reviews. Todd McCarthy of the *Hollywood Reporter*, known to be a brutal critic, loved it. He described it as "a wonderfully entertaining documentary about the club where it all began for many of today's top comic talent."

We went on to screen the documentary at the Just For Laughs comedy festival, the Friars Club Comedy Film

Festival, and the Black Harvest Film Festival. The best of them all, for me, was Roger Ebert's Ebertfest in Chicago. Roger personally selected all of the films, and we were the opening-night feature. It was simply awe-inspiring to watch our film in a sold-out 1,500-seat theater with a state-of-the-art 70-mm, 100-foot screen. When I walked onstage for the Q&A, I got a standing ovation and at least one rave review:

"If the 2012 Ebertfest were to have a real-life hero of a sort, it might be Raymond C. Lambert, a black entrepreneur who founded All Jokes Aside in 1991 in the South Loop in Chicago. Intelligent, accomplished and above-board in a city rife with corruption, Lambert refused to make under-the-table payments a decade later when he moved his comedy club a mile north and met with a delay in getting a liquor license. He stands by the 'integrity of his failure,'" wrote Melissa Merli of the *News-Gazette* in Champaign-Urbana, Illinois.

We also had private screenings in New York, Chicago, and, most notably, on the lot at Hollywood's Paramount Studios in the Sherry Lansing Theatre. Very cool.

Perhaps the coolest thing of all was that Pearlena Igbokwe, Showtime's senior vice president of programming, loved it, and the cable network purchased the film. It premiered on Showtime during Black History Month in 2012.

Many folks asked me how I felt about that. Did premiering during Black History Month marginalize our work? I have no problem with Black History Month. It is what it is. I don't go all-out for Black History Month; black history is American history and should be taught year-round. But I do routinely participate in events during the month each year.

And as far as the documentary was concerned, my thinking was, *Let's use every opportunity to put our best foot forward and roll with it.* The film continues to run on Showtime from time to time, and the network has been very happy with it. The response from all who have seen it has been, for the most part, great.

As good as the film experience was, the best thing to happen to me as a result of doing it was reconnecting again with Chris Gardner. While we had stayed in touch over the years, we had never sat down and really talked. He invited me over to have coffee, and we met half a dozen times after that.

The opportunity to spend more time with Chris was very valuable. At the time, I was definitely starting to have doubts about the PhD path that had seemed like such a great option for me not long before. I had devoted a lot of time to the film, and it had slowed down my path to completing the degree. With my master's degree, I was qualified to teach, which is what truly interested me most about the academic world. Research held less appeal for me than teaching. The more I thought about the PhD, the more it struck me that I would be training to be a consultant. I never wanted to be a consultant. Consultants make recommendations. Entrepreneurs make decisions. I like to make decisions.

Any dream that is truly right for us can't be easily abandoned. If it is truly a calling we should pursue, it returns to us in a new form and asks us to resume the journey. Someone or something snaps us back to attention, and then we're back on our path once again. Re-enter Chris Gardner. I saw it clear as day: *Social entrepreneurship. Conscious capitalist.* When I had interviewed Chris for *Phunny Business*, we had talked briefly about what I wanted to do after the film. He had transitioned out of the securities business and wanted to build a business with the objective of doing well by doing good. He wanted to provide a positive return to investors and have a positive impact on society. But what would that look like?

As I was contemplating this and trying to determine the right direction to take, my marriage had entered a turbulent period as well. In a relatively short period, Schnell and I had experienced the failure of my business, two kids in diapers, and the death of three parents (her father had passed away unexpectedly a year after mine). We were in the middle of a recession that began in 2008, and it was wreaking havoc on the real estate markets; her residential real estate business was not spared. Add it all up, and you had a toxic cocktail of trouble. I hated the idea of divorce, but in an already-strained marriage, there is no tension a business can't make worse. We committed to counseling, but it didn't work. Entrepreneurs start companies to do their own things, while marriage is about doing things together.

Albeit for very different reasons, I became a statistic like my parents. In 2011, after seven years of marriage, we amicably decided to divorce. We remain friends and are soldiers in the daily battle of trying to raise two well-rounded, confident, selfless, caring, and productive citizens.

In the years since I got my start with him in Chicago, Chris had done incredibly well with Gardner Rich. Beyond that, he'd become a celebrity after writing his *New York Times* bestselling memoir, *The Pursuit of Happyness*. More than 1 billion people around the world saw the book's film adaptation. With all of this success under his belt, Chris had reached the point where he wanted to do something more than just make money.

For my part, I was now divorced with two young kids, and I certainly needed to make a living. But I have never been interested in the pursuit of money for money's sake. I am unencumbered by the weight of the expectations of others and the empty pursuit of material wealth. And like Chris, I wanted to find a way to apply everything I had learned and experienced in order to make the world a better place. I wanted to live at the intersection of purpose and profit, offering new ideas for wide-scale change and developing innovative solutions to society's most pressing social problems. I welcomed the idea of working with Chris again—one of the most dynamic entrepreneurs I've ever known.

So here we go, working with Chris and a number of conscience capital-building companies where ideas, people, and capital come together to serve as a catalyst and provide tools for individuals and corporations in pursuit of their own hopes and dreams. We're seeking ventures that produce a triple bottom line by earning a quantifiable return on investment, making a measurable impact on society, and creating jobs.

As Martin Luther King Jr. so famously said, "If a man doesn't have a job or an income, he has neither life nor liberty nor the possibility for the pursuit of happiness. He merely exists."

While conscience capitalism is my primary focus, I am not done with comedy. I am enamored of the idea of utilizing the power of standup for social change. And comedians, in my humble opinion, are the leading arbiters of thought among all entertainers. So let's come together, utilizing our talents to make the world a better place than we found it. When all is said and done, at least for me anyway, it's about being a candle in the dark. In fact, it's all that I ever wanted to be . . . all jokes aside.

ACKNOWLEDGMENTS

I would like to express my sincere gratitude to the many people who saw me through this book: to all those who provided support, talked things over, read, wrote, offered comments, allowed me to quote their remarks, and assisted in the editing, proofreading, and design.

I would like to thank my collaborator, Chris Bournea, for agreeing to take this journey with me. Thank you to Chris Gardner for his experience, wisdom, and perspective during this often-challenging trip. I want to thank Nia Rae Lambert and Maya Jo Lambert, my rocks, who supported and encouraged me in spite of all the time it took me away from them.

I would like to thank Wil Haygood for introducing me to Chris Bournea. I'd also like to thank Stacey Gray, Betty Gray, Rachelle Ray, Kirsten Miccoli, Charles White, and Wayne Beach for helping me in the process of selecting and editing. Thanks to my publisher Doug Seibold, and his team at Agate, who felt that my story was worthy of their attention.

Thanks to the comedians, staff members, and every customer who bought a ticket to see a show at All Jokes Aside. This book would not be possible without you.

I beg forgiveness from all those who have been with me over the course of the years whose names I have failed to mention.

ABOUT THE AUTHORS

RAYMOND LAMBERT is a social entrepreneur, independent producer, and adjunct professor at Columbia College in Chicago. He earned writer and producer credits for the award-winning documentary film *Phunny Business*, and he is an executive producer of the forthcoming documentaries *All the Queen's Horses* (Kartemquin Films) and *Maya Angelou: The People's Poet*. He has been a consultant on comedy and talent to producers at NBC, HBO, Comedy Central, Just For Laughs, and BET. Lambert earned a degree in marketing from Morehouse College and an MBA from the University of Virginia's Darden Graduate School of Business. He lives in Chicago.

CHRIS BOURNEA is a journalist, author, and documentary filmmaker. He began his career at Ohio's historic African American newspaper, the *Call and Post*, and has covered a wide range of stories, from President Barack Obama's historic 2008 election to interviews with numerous bestselling authors. Bournea is the author of the novel *The Chloe Chronicles* and directed the soon-to-be-released documentary *Lady Wrestler: The Amazing, Untold Story of African-American Women in the Ring*.